DATE DUE			
GAYLORD M-2			PRINTED IN U.S.A.

MARRIAGE NOTICES

1785 - 1794

FOR THE

WHOLE UNITED STATES.

COPIED FROM THE MASSACHUSETTS CENTINEL

AND THE COLUMBIAN CENTINEL.

BY

CHARLES KNOWLES BOLTON.

Baltimore
Genealogical Publishing Co.
1965

Originally Published
Salem, Mass., 1900

Library of Congress Catalog Card No. 65-28304

MARRIAGE NOTICES, FOR THE WHOLE UNITED STATES 1785-1794.

COPIED FROM COMPLETE FILES OF THE MASSACHUSETTS CENTINEL AND THE COLUMBIAN CENTINEL, WITH A PREFACE AND OCCASIONAL NOTES.

BY CHARLES KNOWLES BOLTON.

THE marriages recorded in the *Centinel* were of three kinds: those of well-to-do persons, useful to the genealogist because they give in many cases the actual day of the marriage as well as the name of the bride's father and his residence; those of celebrities, like General Gates, and members of the Washington family, sometimes communicated by travellers, and often inaccurate; those of eccentric people, usually amusing.

The date given here is always that of the paper. The marriage may have taken place a day or a month previous to the insertion of the notice. Sometimes the date may be found by reckoning back from the day on which the paper was issued to the day of the week on which the marriage took place, if the day is given. W. in the following records stands for Wednesday and S. for Saturday. "In this town" refers to Boston, Mass.

The third class of notices illustrates one side of the old time New England life, a love of the grotesque and the unusual. The space now devoted to sensational trials was filled one hundred years ago, with accounts of people of great age and the number of their living descendants, of marriages of curious characters, of deaths by loathsome diseases, and of the ingenious punishments inflicted on unlucky criminals.

The unusual number of printers noticed shows the fraternal feeling which has always characterized the press.

I have taken no liberties with proper names, except misprints of the most familiar given names. It should be borne in mind that names were as a rule printed in small caps, and the confusion of letters like E and N and L is common.

Without the kindly assistance of those connected with Bates Hall, in the Boston Public Library, I could not, with my slight leisure, have found time for the undertaking.

Abbot, Anna, m. Knot Martin, 3d.

Abbot, Patty, m. Joseph Jenks.

Abbot, Solomon, at Andover, Mr. S. A. to Miss Lucy Fry. (S. July 12, 1794.)

Abell, Hannah, m. Wheeler Coit.

Aborn, Polly, m. Capt. Thomas Hollis Condy.

Adams, Elijah, Mr. E. A. to Miss Judith Townsend, of this town, (S. Oct. 24, 1789.)

Adams, John, Mr. J. A. to Miss Fanny Cowing. (S. Oct. 11, 1788.)

Adams, Joseph, Mr. J. A. of Litchfield, to Miss Deborah Marsh, of that place. (S. Feb. 18, 1792.)

Adams, Mary, m. John Bright.

Adams, Mary, m. Hon. George Taylor Gilman.

Adams, Nancy, m. Nathaniel F. Cunningham.

Adams, Polly, m. Col. Edward Proctor.

Adams, Ruth, m. Samuel L. Parker.

Adams, Ruthy, m. Michael Mallet.

Adams, Sally, m. William Johnson.

Adams, Seth. By the Rev. Mr. Freeman, Mr. S. A. to Miss Elizabeth Apthrop, eldest daughter of the late Mr. William Apthrop. (S. Feb. 8, 1794.)

Adams, Sukey, m. John Vinal.

Adams, Thomas, Mr. T. A., printer, to Miss Polly Bright, daughter to Mr. George Bright. (W. Oct. 21, 1789.)

Addison, John, at Epping, (Mary.) J. A. Esq. to Miss Sarah Leitch. (S. Oct. 27, 1792.)

Akin, Capt. William, at Darmouth, Capt. W. A. to Miss Hannah Howland. (S. March 9, 1793.)

Akins, Polly, m. Glover Mansfield.

Albro, John, at Halifax, Mr. J. A. to Miss Elizabeth Vandegret. (S. Nov. 23, 1793.)

Alcot, Polly, m. Samuel Homes.

Alden, Caleb, Mr. C. A. to Miss Sally Hayward. (S. Feb. 26, 1791.)

Alden, Eliza, m. David Thomas.

Alexander, Joseph, in this town, Mr. J. A. to Miss Nabby Weare, [both] of this town. (S. Nov. 6, 1790.)

Alger, Thomas, in this town, Mr. M. A. to Miss Elizabeth Robinson. (S. Aug. 23, 1794.)

Allbee, Capt. at Roxbury, Capt. A. of Mendon, to Mrs. Bugbee, of Roxbury. (S. Aug. 28, 1790.)

Allen, B., jun., at Tisbury, (M. V.) Mr. B. A. jun., to Miss Nabby Morse. (W. Oct. 27, 1790.)

Allen, Daniel, at Colrain, Mr. D. A. to Miss Nancy Stewart, daughter of John Stewart, of Shelburn. (W. March 13, 1793.)

Allen, Grace, m. John Davis.

Allen, Dea. Joseph, at Hardwick, Dea J. A., aged 80, to Mrs. Knowlton, aged 50. (S. Aug. 22, 1789.)

Allen, Joseph, at Hinsdale, Mr. J. A. of Worcester, to Miss Fanny Jones, of Hinsdale. (S. April 5, 1794.)

Allen, Josiah, jun. in this town, Mr. J. A. jun. to Miss Hannah Hartwick. (S. May 29, 1790.)

Allen, Oliver, Mr. O. A. to Miss Susanna Whitman. (S. Feb. 26, 1791.)

Allen, Peggy, m. William Bruce.

Allen, Peggy, m. George Hammond.

Allen, Polly, m. Capt. Josiah Edes.

Allen, Rebecca, m. Capt. William Bullock.

Allen, Samuel, in this town, Mr. S. A. to Miss Patty Trask. (S. Nov. 24, 1792.)

Alline, William, in this town, Mr. W. A. to Miss Rebecca Cazneau. (W. July 16, 1794.)

Almy, Katy, m. Edmund Trowbridge Ellery.

Alsop, Clarissa, m. Major Samuel W. Pomeroy.

Ames, Miss, m. Rev. Samuel Shuttleworth.

Ames, Hon. Fisher, at Springfield, Hon. F. A., Esq. member of Congress, to Miss Frances Worthington. (5 July 28, 1792.)

Amory, Catherine, m. John Codman, jun.

Amory, Elizabeth, m. Stephen Deblois.

Amory, Francis, in this town, on Sunday evening last, Mr. F. A. to the beautiful Miss Prudence Eustis. (W. Dec. 12, 1792.)

Amory, John, jun., at Lancaster, Mr. J. A. jun., of this town, to the agreeable Miss Catherine Willard. (W. Feb. 1, 1792.)

Amory, Jonathan, in this town, Mr. J. A. merchant, to Miss Lydia Fellows, only child of Mr. Nathaniel Fellows, merchant of this place. (S. Oct. 25, 1794.)

Amory, Rufus G., in this town, R. J. A. Esq. attorney at law, to Miss

Nancy Geyer; daughter to Frederick N. Geyer, Esq. (S. Feb. 15, 1794.)

Anderson, Joseph, at Freeport, Mr. J. A. to Miss Kendall. (S. Oct. 11, 1794.)

Audrews, Ebenezer T., in this town, Mr. E. T. A., printer, to Miss Weld, both of this town. (S. Dec. 24, 1791.)

Andrews, Rev. John, at Cambridge, by the Rev. Mr. Hilliard, the Rev. J. A., of Newbury-port, to Miss Peggy Wigglesworth, daughter of Dr. Edward Wigglesworth, Professor of Divinity in the University at Cambridge. (S. Sept. 12, 1789.)

Andrews, Capt. John, at Windsor, N. S., Capt. J. A. to Miss Catherine Scott. (S. July 6, 1793.)

Andrews Mindwell, m. Simon Hastings.

Andrews, Sally, m. John Sweetser Lillie.

Andrews, Samuel, in this town, Mr. S. A. to Miss Betsy Urann. (W. Dec. 26, 1792.)

Andrews, Samuel, at Hingham, Mr. S. A. of Worcester, to Miss Katy Cushing, of Hingham. (S. Jan. 11, 1794.)

Andrews, William, in this town, Mr. W. A. to Miss Polly Stutson. (W. Nov. 30, 1791.)

Angel, Miss, m. William Goddard.

Angier, Hannah, m. William Taylor.

Angier, Ruthy, m. Oliver Wiswall.

Angier, Dr. Samuel, at Taunton, Dr. S. A. to Miss Carver, both of that place. (S. Nov. 10, 1792.)

Annis, Elizabeth, m. Joseph Mansfield.

Anthony, Ruth, m. Nathan Spencer.

Applegate, Kitty, m. Archibald Thompson.

Appleton, Eliza, m. Bartholomew Carter.

Appleton, John, Mr. J. A., merchant, of Salem, to Miss Greenleaf, daughter to William Greenleaf, Esq. of this town. (S. March 22, 1794.)

Appleton, Nathaniel, m. Thomas Perkins.

Appleton, Polly, m. Samuel Emery.

Apthorp, Miss, m. Hon. Hugh Williamson.

Apthorp, Frances Weston, m. Charles Vaugham.

Apthorp, Hannah, m. Charles Bulfinch.

Apthorp, Lucy Ann, m. Richard Nash.

Apthrop, Charles, at St. John's, (N. B.) C. A., Esq., Lieut. in his Britannick Majesty's Navy, to Miss Mary Prince. (S. Aug. 21, 1790.)

Apthrop, Elizabeth, m. Seth Adams.

Archbald, Azor G., Mr. A. G. A. to Miss Lucretia May, both of this town. (S. May 5, 1787.)

Army, Betsy, m. John Bolier. Almy?

Arnold, Eliza, m. Jesse Fenns.

Arnold, Capt. John, at Providence, Capt. J. A. to Mrs. Abigail Throop. (S. March 17, 1792.)

Arnold, Lydia, m. Jeremiah Green.

Arsonneau, Peter Remy, last Tuesday evening was married, by the Rev. Mr. Stilman, Mr. P. R. A. to Miss Ruth Homer, she was a daughter of Benjamin Homer. (W. June 15, 1785.)

Aslop, Abby, m. Theodore Dwight.

Aspinwall, Mr., at Watertown, Mr. A. of Brooklyn, to Miss Anna Chinery, of Watertown.
John Aspinwall of Brookline.

Aspinwall, Caleb, Mr. C. A. to Miss Betsey Freeman, eldest daughter of Mr. Phillip Freeman, jun., deceased. (S. April 9, 1785.)

Aspinwall, Sally, m. Col. Richard Platt.

Atkins, Abigail, m. John W. Quincy.

Atkins, Hannah, m. Col. Edward Proctor.

Atkins, Katherine, m. Samuel Eliot.

Atkins, Martha, m. Capt. Robert Gray.

Atwater, John, at Charlestown, Mr. J. A. to Miss Martha Call. (S. Feb. 2, 1793.)

Atwood, Polly, m. John Broadbroker.

Atwood, Sally, m. John Bonon Graves.

Atwood, Susanna, m. Thomas Williams.

Atwood, Zacariah, at Newbury-port, Mr. Z. A. to Miss Peggy Ford. (S. July 6, 1793.)

Austin, Benjamin, jun., last evening, Mr. B. A. jun., merchant, to the amiable Miss Jane Ivers, daughter of James Ivers, Esq. of this town. (W. July 27, 1785.)

Austin, Betsy m. John Brown.

Austin, Daniel, Mr. D. A. of this town, merchant, to Miss Polly Penhallow, of Portsmouth. (S. Aug. 4, 1787.)

Austin, Grace, m. Samuel Hill.

Austin, Samuel, Mr. S. A. to Miss Nabby Lewis, both of this town. (W. Nov. 17, 1790.)

Avery, Mrs., m. John Jackson.

Avery, Eliza, m. William Eldridge.

Avery, Polly, m. Luke Baldwin.

Avery, Sally, m. Coffin Johnson.

Ayers, Nancy, m. Thomas Hearsy.

Ayers, Nathaniel, Mr. N. A. to Miss Katy Gardner. (S. March 7, 1789.)

Ayres, Henry, in this town, Mr. H. A. to Miss Hepsey Cooledge, both of this town. (W. Nov. 26, 1794.)

Babbidge, Patty, m. Andrew Ward.

Bache, Benjamin Franklin, at Philadelphia, Mr. B. F. B. printer, to Miss Markoe. (S. Dec. 3, 1791.)

Bache, Paul R. at New-York, Mr. P. R. B. to Miss Helen Lispenard, eldest daughter of Anthony Lispenard, Esq. of that city. (W. Nov. 14, 1792.)

Bacon, Mrs., m. Hon. Thomas Smith.

Bacon, Keziah, m. Capt. Thomas Buckminster.

Bacon, Thomas, in this town, Mr. T. B. of New-York, to Miss Mary Guerney, of this town. (W. Oct. 31, 1792.)

Badger, Thomas, at Charlestown, last Sunday evening, Mr. T. B. of this town, to Miss Nabby Newell, daughter of Capt. Eliphalet Newell, of that town. (Sat. July 8, 1786.)

Bailey, Calvin, at Scituate, Mr. C. B., of Hanover, to Mrs. Sarah Jacobs. (W. Sept. 14, 1793.)

Bailey, Loring, Mr. L. B. to Miss Polly Parker, [both] of this town. (S. Aug. 6, 1789.)

Baily, William. In Rhode Island, Mr. W. B., to Miss Sally Irish. (W. Dec. 26, 1792.)

Baker, Abigail, m. Josiah Bumstead.

Baker, Alexander, in this town, on Sunday evening last, Mr. A. B., to Mrs. Mary Rose. (W. Mch. 9, 1791.)

Baker, Bethiah, m. Ephraim Copeland.

Baker, Edmund, at Dorchester, on Thursday evening, Mr. E. B. to Miss Sally How. (S. Oct. 1, 1791.)

Baker, Marcey L., m. John Ford.

Baker, Nancy, m. Nicholas Durivage.

Baker, Priscilla, m. Samuel Mosely.

Balch, Joseph, jun., [in this town] Mr. J. B. jun., to Miss Hannah Pope. (W. Oct. 8, 1794.)

Balch, Mary, m. Benjamin Morgan Stillman.

Balch, Nabby, m. Capt. Peter Bright.

Balch, Nathaniel, jun., Mr. N. B. jun., to Miss Mary Stillman. (S. Dec. 19, 1789.)

Balding Mr , [at New York] Mr. B. to Miss Mary Dodge. (W. June 13, 1792.)

Baldwin, Mrs., m. Rev. Eli Forbes.

Baldwin, Loamni, at Woburn, L. B., Esq., to Miss Margaret Fowle. (W. June 15, 1791.)

Baldwin, Luke. Last evening by the Rev. Mr. Howard, Mr. L. B., of Brookfield, to Miss Polly Avery, daughter of John Avery, jun., Esq., of this town. (W. Sept. 9, 1789.)

Baldwin, Methusala, at New-Ark, Mr. B., preacher of the Gospel, to Miss Jane Higgins. (W. May 16, 1792.)

Ballou, Silas, at Gloucester, (R. I.), Mr. S. B. aged 18, to Miss Pray, aged 15 years, both only children of respectable parents. One source of wealth to a young country, said Dr. Franklin, is early marrying. (W. Oct. 1, 1794.)

Bancroft, Rev. Aaron, at Worcester, the Rev. A. B. to Miss Lucretia Chandler, daughter of the Hon. John Chandler, Esq. (S. Oct. 28, 1786.)

Bangs, Edward, at Worcester, E. B., Esq., attorney at law, to Miss Hannah Lyndes. (S. Sept. 27, 1788.)

Bangs, Elisha, Mr. E. B. to Miss Nancy Greenough, both of this town. (S. Nov. 4, 1786.)

Bangs, Sally, m. Daniel Rea, tertius.

Bangs, Samuel, jun., Mr. S. B. jun., to Miss Hannah Grice. (W. Nov. 5, 1788.)

Barber, Catherine Macaulay, m. John Osborne.

Barber, Polly, m. Ebenezer White.

Bard, Nancy, m. Col. Pierce.

Bard, S., m. John Johnston.

Barker, Lemuel, [at Dartmouth], Mr. L. B. to Miss Maria Tripe, both of Dartmouth. (S. Dec. 7, 1793.)

Barker, Polly, m. Thomas Smith, jun.

Barker, Mrs. Sarah, m. Jorden Rexford.

Barksdale, Susannah Frances, m. Major Edward Phelon.

Barnard, Abigail, m. Capt. Joshua Clapp.

Barnard, Betsy, m. Enoch Brown.

Barnard, Polly, m. Thomas Blake.

Barnard, Rachel, m. Hart Leavit.

Barnard, Sally, m. Dr. Stone.

Barnard, Tristram, [at Nantucket] Mr. T. B. to Miss Phebe Swain. (W. July 17, 1793.)

Barnes, Jacob, at Marlborough, Mr. J. B. to Miss Hipzabath Howe, daughter of Mr. Joseph Howe. (S. Jan. 19, 1793.)

Barnes, Miles. In this town Mr. M. B., to Miss Peggy Orr, both of this town. (W. Jan. 11, 1786.)

Barnes, William, at Roxbury on Thursday evening last, Mr. W. B. to Miss Jenny Thompson. (S. Dec. 1, 1792.)

Barnett, William. In this town, by the Rev. Dr. Walters, W. B. Esq., of the island of Jamaica, to the accomplished and agreeable Miss Aby Norwood, of this town. (W. Nov. 21, 1792.)

Barnum, Priscilla, m. Capt. David Vickery.

Barret, Nathaniel, at New York, Mr. N. B. of this town, to Mrs. McDougal, relict of the late Major-General McDougal, of that city. (W. Jan. 7, 1789.)

Barrett, Isaac. Mr. I. B., to Miss Hannah M'Niel. (S. Dec. 13, 1788.)

Barrett, John, at Northfield, 29th ult., J. B., Esq., Attorney at Law, to the amiable Miss Patty Dickinson, both of that place. (S. Nov. 13, 1790.)

Barrett, Joseph, jun. Mr. J. B., jun., to Miss Deborah Webb, both of this town. (S. Aug. 6, 1791.)

Barrett, Martha, m. Samuel Sumner.

Barrett, Nancy, m. Dr. Isaac Green.

Barrett, Sarah, m. Dr. Boucher Leonard.

Barron, Lydia, m. David Hill.

Barry, Betsey, m. Elijah Leavitt.

Barry, James, Mr. J. B., to Miss Mehitable Crane. (S. April 2, 1791.)

Barry, Thomas. in this town, Mr. T. B., to Miss Sally Cushing. (W. March 20, 1793.)

Bartholomew, Miss, m. Henry Capper.

Bartlett, Abel, [at Newburyport] Mr. A. B. to Miss Bridget Smith. W. Jan. 15, 1794.)

Bartlett, Bailey, at Haverhill, on Tuesday, the 21st ult., by the Rev. Hezekiah Smith, B. B., Esq., to Miss White, only daughter of Mr. John White, merchant. (S. Dec. 2, 1786.)

Bartlett, George, at Charlestown, on Sunday evening last, Mr. G. B., to Miss Mary Gorham, second daughter to Mr. Nathaniel Gortham, Esq. (W. Oct. 15, 1794.)

Bartlett, Dr. John, at Roxbury, last evening, Dr. J. B., to Miss Abigail Williams. (W. Feb. 18, 1789.)

Bartlett, John, at Newbury-Port, Mr. J. B., to Miss Jane Carr. (W. April, 18, 1792.)

Bartlett, Polly, m. Eleazer Homer.

Bartlett, Thomas, [in this town] Mr. T. B., to Mrs. Alice Wyer. (S. Feb. 15, 1794.)

Barton, Lillis, m. Ansell Churchill.

Barton, Sally, m. Capt. John Derby.

Barton, Susan, m. Caleb Clipton.

Barton, Rev. Titus Theodore. The Rev. T. T. B., of Tewesbury, to Mrs. Ruth Wood of Methuen, widow of the late Rev. Jacob Wood, of Newbury, Vermont. (W. Aug. 6, 1794.)

Barton, William, [in this town] Mr. W. B., to Miss Hannah Scott. (S. Feb. 23, 1793.)

Bartram, Betsey, m. Eden Palmer.

Barcom, Rev. Mr. At Long-meadow, Rev. Mr. B., to Miss Patty Reynolds, and Rev. Mr. Kinsbury to Miss Polly Reynolds, sisters. (W. Feb. 22, 1792.)

Bascom, Mercy, m. Israel Phillips.

Bass, Rev. Dr., at Newbury-Port, Rev. Dr. B., to Miss Mary Phillips. (W. Dec. 2, 1789.)

Bass, Faith, m. Samuel S. Wheeler.

Bass, William, in this town, Mr. W. B., to Miss Sally Loring. (S. May 18, 1793.)

Baty, Rachel, m. George Blake.

Baty, Mrs. Thankful, m. Joseph Blake.

Baxter, John. On Sunday last, Mr. J. B., to Miss Betsey Marshall, both of this town. (W. Sept. 29, 1790.)

Baxter, Joseph, [in this town] Mr. J. B., to Miss Nancy Dashwood. (S. Nov. 29, 1794.)

Bayle, Kiah, at Harvard, K. B., A. B. candidate for the ministry of religion to Miss Abigail Goodhue, formerly of Newburyport. Married Oct. 2. (W. Oct. 8, 1794.)

Bayley, Abigail, m. John Fox.

Bayley, Cazneau, at Newburyport, Mr. C. B., to Miss Elizabeth Newell. (W. April 12, 1794.)

Beal, Christopher, [in this town] Mr. C. B. Housewright, to Miss Mary Downs, both of this town. (S. May 12, 1792.)

Beale, Theodosia, m. Capt. John Willson Chorley.

Beals, Jenny, m. Joseph Robertson.

Beals, Patty, m. Zeabilon Hall.

Beaty, Capt. Thomas. In Georgetown (M.) Capt. T. B., mar. to Miss Harrison. (W. Feb. 29, 1792.)

Beaujean, Moses, [at Portsmouth] Mr. M. B. to Miss Rebecca Furniss. (S. Nov. 15, 1794.)

Beck, Johanna, m. George Ham.

Beck, Mrs. Sarah, m. Hon. William Phillips.

Becket, Nabby, m. Benjamin Hawks.

Beckley, John, at New York, J. B., Esq., Clerk of the House of Representatives of the United States, to Miss Maria Prince, of that city. (W. Oct. 27, 1790.)

Bedlington, Thomas, Mr. T. B: of London, to Miss Polly Moody, daughter to Deacon Moody, of this town. (W. Nov. 4, 1789.)

Bedlow, Mary Elizabeth Good, m. John Beckman.

Bedon, Wesson, at Dartmouth, Mr. W. B. to Miss Sybel Wood. (W. Dec. 25, 1793.)

Beekman, Elizabeth, m. Peter W. Livingston.

Beekman, John, at New-York, J. B., Esq., to Miss Mary Elizabeth Goad Bedlow. (W. Nov. 21, 1792.)

Beequet (?), Francis B., at Newbury-Port, Mr. F. B. B., to Miss Sally Wigglesworth. (W. Sept. 25, 1793.)

Belcher, Miss, m. Dr. J. Jennison.

Belcher, Andrew, in this town, by Rev. Dr. Stillman, Mr. A. B., of Halifax, to Miss Marianne Geyer, daughter to Frederick W. Geyer, Esq. (W. Sept. 12, 1792.)

Belcher, Debby, m. Edward Reynolds.

Bell, Sally, m. Daniel Carney.

Bell, Shubael, last Sunday evening, Mr. S. B., to Miss Betsy Robinson. (W. March 19, 1788.)

Bennet, Deborah, m. William Eustis.

Bennet, Thomas, at Middleborough, Mr. T. B. to Miss Ruthy Thompson, daughter of Capt. Jacob Thompson, of that place. (S. Aug. 24, 1793.)

Bennett, Sarah, m. N. Fairchild.

Benny, Lucy, m. Caleb Lambert.

Benny, Sally, m. Elijah Trask.

Benson, George, at Providence, Mr. G. B. to Miss Sally Thurber. (W. Feb. 6, 1793.)

Bentley, Polly, m. Reuben Dawes.

Bently, Betsy, m. Henry Fowle.

Bernald, Hannah, m. Joseph Keen.

Berrett, Polly, m. Jacob Nice.

Berry, Sally, m. Micajah Johnson.

Bethune, Jenny, m. William Hunt.

Bicker, Sally, m. William Walter.

Bidwell, Barnabas, at Watertown, B. B., Esq., to Miss Polly Gray, both of Stockbridge. (S. March 16, 1793.)

Bigelow, Timothy, at Groton, T. B., Esq., attorney at law, to the truly amiable Miss Prescot, daughter to the Hon. Oliver Prescot, Esq., of that town. (W. Oct. 12, 1791.)

Billings, Betsey, m. John Langley, jun.

Bingham, Caleb, last Monday evening, Mr. C. B. to Miss Hannah Kimball, both of this town. (W. Feb. 1, 1786.)

Bingham, Liscomb, [at Westborough] Mr. L. B., to Miss Patty Fay. (W. Dec. 19, 1792.)

Binney, Mrs., m. Dr. Marshall Spring.

Binney, Avis, m. Nicholas Brown.

Bird, Clarissa, m. Christopher Ellery.

Bishop, Abraham, at Newbury-Port, A. B., Esq., of New-Haven, to Miss Nancy Dexter, of Newbury-Port. (W. March 14, 1792.)

Bishop, Nabby, m. Dr. Archelaus Putnam.

Bixby, Mrs. Ruth, m. Capt. Jeremiah Shattuck.

Black, Betsey, m. William Heath.

Black, Anna, m. Joseph Blake, jun.

Blackler, William, at Marblehead, M. W. B., to Miss Eliza Gerry, eldest daughter of Samuel R. Gerry. (W. May 8, 1793.)

Blackman, Andrew, at Watertown, Mr. A. B., to Miss Sally White, of that town. (W. Feb. 18, 1789.)

Blagge, Samuel, Mr. S. B., merchant, to Miss Sally Hall, daughter of Mr. Stephen Hall, of this town. (W. Dec. 13, 1786.)

B'ake, Betsy, m. William Williams.

Blake, Edward, in this town, Mr. E. B., to Mrs. Sally Underwood. (W. Oct. 3, 1792.)

Blake, Francis, at Lancaster, Mr. F. B., of Rutland, attorney at law, to Miss Eliza Augusta Chandler, of the first mentioned place. (W. Dec. 17, 1794.)

Blake, George, in this town, Mr. G. B., attorney at law, to Miss Rachel Baty. (S. Jan. 18, 1794.)

Blake, Joseph, Mr. J. B., member of the legislature from Milton, to Mrs. Thankful Baty, of this town. (S. May 23, 1789.)

Blake, Joseph, jun., in this town, J. B. jun., Esq., to Miss Anna Black. (W. Jan. 9, 1793.)

Blake, Polly, m. Samuel Ruggles.

Blake, Rebecca, m. Stephen Bruce.

Blake, Reuben, on Thursday, at Dorchester, Mr. R. B. to Miss Betsy Peirce, daughter to Col. Samuel Peirce. (S. Oct. 15, 1791.)

Blake, Susannah, m. William Seaver.

Blake, Thomas, in this town, Mr. T. B. to Miss Polly Barnard. (S. Feb. 23, 1793.)

Blake, William, in this town, Mr. W. B., to Miss Deborah Breck. (S. July 31, 1790.)

Blake, William, in this town, Mr. W. B., to Miss Sally Gendell, both of this town. (S. April 21, 1792.)

Blake, Major Ziba, at Milton, Major Z. B., to Miss Susannah Tucker. (S. Feb. 12, 1791.)

Blanchard, Francis, [in this town] Mr. F. B., to Miss Hannah Whipple, both of this town. (S. April 19, 1794.)

Blanchard, George, in this town, Mr. G. B., to Miss Betsy Tilden. (S. June 22, 1793.)

Blanchard, John W., [in this town] Mr. J. W. B. to Miss Abigail Dalton. (W. April 17, 1793.)

Blanchard, Sarah, m. Francis Childs.

Blanton, James, at Cheraw, S. C., Mr. J. B., aged 65, to Miss Martha Smith, aged 12. (S. June 30, 1792.)

Blish, Joseph, at Barnstable, Mr. J. B., to Miss Temperance Shaw, daughter [of] the Rev. Mr. Shaw. (W. July 22, 1789.)

Blin, Ebenezer, at Great-Barrington, Mr. E. B., to Miss Lucy Porter. (S. Feb. 9, 1793.)

Bliss, Experience, m. John Chaloner.

B ss, Hon. Jonathan, at Springfield, Hon. J. B., Esq., of the Province of New-Brunswick, to Miss Mary Worthington, daughter of the Hon. John Worthington, Esq. (S. July 17, 1790.)

Bliss, Peletiah, at Springfield, Mr. P. B., to Miss Polly Stebbins. (S. Nov. 22, 1794.)

Blodget, Samuel, jun., at Philadelphia, Mr. S. B. jun., of this town, to Miss Rebecca Smith, daughter of the Rev. Dr. Wm. Smith, of that city. (W. May 23, 1792.)

Blunt, Edmund M., at New-York, Mr. E. M. B., printer, of Newburyport, to Miss Sarah Ross, of Marblehead. (W. June 11, '1794.)

Boardman, Susannah, m. Joshua Reed.

Boardman, Capt. William, on Thursday evening, by the Rev. Samuel West, Capt. W. B., to Miss Sally Davis, eldest daughter of Colonel Amasa Davis, of this town. (S. May 28, 1791.)
Deaths: In this town, yesterday, Mrs. Sally Bordman, wife of Capt. William Bordman. (S. June 30, 1792.)

Boardman, see also Bordman.

Bo lge, Edward, in this town, Mr. E. B., to Miss Anna Meriam. (S. Jan. 19, 1793.)

Bo ly, Olive, m. George Johnson.

Bogart, David S., at New-York. D. S. B., Esq., to Miss Elizabeth Platt. (W. May 16, 1792.)

Boib, Hannah, m. Crowel Hatch.

Boib, Sally, m. John Dubalett.

Boles, Sally, m. George Frost.

Bolles, John, Mr. J. B. to Miss Betsey Army [Almy?] at New-London implied. (S. April 14, 1792.)

Bolter, Benjamin, Mr. B. B. to Miss Peggy Moggin. (W. July 6, '91.)

Bond, Amos, at Waltham, A. B. Esq., of Watertown, to Mrs. Abigail Livermore, of Waltham. (S. July 14, 1792.)

Bond, Joseph, in this town, Mr. J. B., of Watertown, to Miss Ruthy Chittendon, of Scituate. (W. Nov. 19. 1794.)

Bonner, John, Mr. J. B., to Miss Abi h Homer, of this town. (S. May 31, 1788.)

Boone, Thomas, [at North-Kingston] Mr. T. B. to Miss Lucy Gardiner. (W. Oct. 8, 1794.)

Bordman, Capt. William, last Thursday evening, Capt. W. B., to Miss Elizabeth Davis, amiable daughter of the Hon. Caleb Davis, Esq., of this town. (S. June 4, 1785.)

Died—yesterday afternoon, Mrs. Elizabeth Bordman, wife of Capt. William Bordman, jun., and the eldest daughter of the Hon. Caleb Davis, Esq. (W. Dec. 15, 1790.)

Bordman, William, [in this town] Mr. W. B., merchant, to Miss Lydia Osborn. (S. June 14, 1794.)

Bordman, see also Boardman.

Borland, Leonard Vassall, last evening, Mr. L. V. B., to Miss Lloyd, only daughter of Doctor James Lloyd, of this town. (W. Feb. 9, 1785.)

Borroughs, William, by the Rev. Mr. Thatcher, Mr. W. B. to the agreeable Miss Sarah Whittemore, both of this town. (W. Feb. 22, 1786.)

Bosworth, Betsey, m. Capt. Clark Drew.

Botting, John, at Ipswich, Mr. J. B., of Concord, to Miss Polly Whipple, of that place. (W. March 19, '94.)

Bourne, Nabby, m. Ebenezer Moulton.

Bourne, Nancy, m. N. W. Otis.

Powden, Sarah, m. Edward Fettiplace.

Bowen, Polly, m. Heman Peirce.

Bowers, Isaac, in this town, Mr. I. B., merchant, to Miss Polly Eyres. (W. May 23 '92.)

Bowers, Mrs. Mariann, m. James Duane, jun.

Bowers, William H., at Swanzey, W. H. B., to Miss Patty Hall, of Connecticut. (W. April 29, '89.)

Bowes, Lydia, m. William B. Procter.

Bowland, Capt. Benjamin, last Sunday evening, Capt. B. B. to Miss Isabella Sinclair, both of this town. (W. May 29, '93.)

Bowland, Mrs. Hannah, m. Joseph Lovering.

Bowles, N., at Petersburg, (Virg.), Mr. N. B., to Miss Mary Minitree. (W. Feb. 29, '92.)

Bowne, Robert L., at Newport, Mr. R. L. B., merchant of New-York, to Miss Almy Robinson. (W. Dec. 18, '93.)

Box, Mary, see Richard Skillings.

Boyd, Miss, m. Capt. John Mackay.

Boyd, Bathuel, the same week, " after a long and tedious courtship," B.

H., of Franklin, Adjutant of the 5th regiment, to the accomplished Miss Sukey Whiting, of Wrentham. (S. Feb. 26, '91.)

Boyd, Frances, m. William Little.

Boyd, Robert, at Portland, Mr. R. B., merchant, to Miss Ruth Smith. (S. Nov. 26, '91.)

Boyd, Samuel, [at Newark] S. B., Esq., of New-York, to Miss Betsy Pierson, of Newark. (W. March 6, 93.)

Boyd, Submit, m. John Samuel Sherburne.

Boyd, William, W. B. Esq., to Miss Susannah Martin, eldest daughter of Thomas Martin, Esq., at Portsmouth implied. (S. Dec. 18, 90.)

Boyd, William, Mr. W. B., to Miss Furman, at New-York implied. (W. April 18, '92.)

Boylston, Miss, m. Dea. Ephraim Frost.

Boylston, William, [in this town] Mr. W. B., to Miss Hannah Gotte. (S. Oct. 27, '92.)

Brabiner, William, [at Halifax], Mr. W. B., to Miss Jane Moody. (W. Nov. 7, '92.)

Bracco, Dr. John, at Easton, (Talbot county) Dr. J. B., to Miss Henrietta Nicholson, both of Queen Ann's county. (W. April 25, '92.)

Brackenridge, Hugh H., at Philadelphia, H. H. B., Esquire, a celebrated counsellor, to Miss Sabina Wolf, a young girl of obscure German parents, on the waters of the Ohio; and has brought her to that city, to spend the ensuing winter, and receive the advantage of some education. (S. Sept. 11, '90.)

> 'Tis easy to admire the flower
> With which the gard'ner deck'd his bow'r;
> Because it must be excellent or rare,
> Before his judgment could have plac'd it there
> But not so easy, in a wood or vale,
> The virtues of a plant or flower to tell—
> Discern its proper class—pronounce its name,
> Select it thence, without least fear or blame,
> And say it has a right better place and fame.

Bracket, Polly, m. George Odiorne.

Brackett, Benjamin, by the Rev. Mr. West, Mr. B. B., to Miss Hannah Davis, eldest daughter of Robert Davis, Esq. (W. July 20, '91.)

Bradbury, Catherine F., m. Ebenezer Clough.

Bradbury, Harriet, m. Thomas Hooper.

Bradford, Dorcas, m. Silas Noyes.

Bradford, Gamaliel, Esq., of Duxbury, to Miss Sukey Tillie. (W. Dec. 1,' 90.)

Bradford, Gamaliel, jun., in this town, Mr. G. B., jun., of Duxborough, to Miss Elizabeth Parker Hickling, of this town. (S. Aug. 11, '92.)

Bradish, Susannah, m. Eliphalet Newell.

Bradlee, David, jun., in this town, Mr. D. B., jun., to Miss Betsey Fellows. (S. Nov. 8, 1788.)

Bradlee, John W., in this town, Mr. J. W B., to Sally Hunnewell. (S. June 15, 1893.)

Bradlee, Josiah, by the Rev. Dr. Stillman, Mr. J. B., to Miss Lydia Callender. (W. Dec. 4, '93.)

Bradlee, Sally, m. Capt. Patrick Fletcher.

Bradley, Stephen, on Monday evening, Mr. S. B., of Milton, to the agreeable and accomplished Miss Sally Davenport, of Stoughton. (S. June 25, '91.)

Bradshaw, Elizabeth, m. Jacobus Pick.

Bradshaw, John, at Albany, Mr. J. B., merchant, of Halfmon, to Miss Rebecca Knickabacker. (W. Aug. 29, '92.)

Bragg, Abiel, at Winslow, Mr. A. B., to Miss Elizabeth Bran. (S. March 2, '93.)

Bran, Elizabeth, m. Abiel Bragg.

Bray, John, on Thursday evening last, Mr. J. B., to Miss Sally Chapman. (S. Nov. 12, '85.)

Bray, Robert, at Salem, Mr. R. B., to Miss Sally Ropes. (W. April 4, '92.)

Breck, Deborah, m. William Blake.

Breck, Helena Dorr, m. Aaron Wright, jun.

Breed, John, [in this town] Mr. J. B., to Miss Polly Hall. (S. June 15, '93.)

Breese, Miss, m. Rev. Jedediah Morse.

Brewer, Dr. Abraham, [at New-York] Dr. A. B., to Miss Eliza Stoutenbourg. (W. Nov. 5, '94.)

Brewer, Ebenezer, at Roxbury, on Christmas eve, by the Rev. Mr. Porter, Mr. E. B., to Miss Polly Foster. (S. Dec. 27, '94.)

Brewer, Capt. John, at St. Stevens, (N. B.), Capt. J. B., to Miss Hannah Marks, of that place. (S. July 20, '93.)

Brewer, Sally, m. William Marean.

Brewer, Samuel, at Northfield, Mr. S. B., merchant, to Miss Sally Norton, of that place. (S. Feb. 18, '92.)

Brewer, Thomas, at Roxbury, Mr. T. B., merchant, to Miss Hannah H. Cazneau, [both of this town.] (S. Nov. 6, '90.)

Brewster, Oliver, Mr. O. B., merchant, to Miss Nancy Ivers, daughter of the late Thomas Ivers, Esq. (S. Dec. 29, '87.)

Bridge, Abigail, m. Thomas Rogers.

Bridge, Hon. Ebenezer, on Thursday evening last, the Hon. E. B. Esq., of Chelmsford, to the amiable Mrs. Mary Mountfort, of this town, relict of Mr. Jonathan Mountfort. (S. Jan. 27, '87.)
In the Centinel—Died on Wednesday last week, at Chelmsford, after a lingering illness, Mrs. Mary Bridge, consort of the Hon. Ebenezer Bridge, Esq., and late the widow of Dr. Jonathan Mountforth, of this town. (W. Sept. 29, '87.)

Bridge, Martha, m. Arthur Lithgou.

Bridges, Hannah, m. Deacon Moses Hall.

Brigham, Elijah, Mr. E. B., of Westborough, merchant, to Mrs. Sally Hamock, of Northborough, relict of Mr. Charles Hamock, late of this town, deceased. (S. May 6, '86.)

Brigham, Elijah, at Shrewsbury, E. B. Esq., to Miss Sarah Ward, daughter to the Hon. Artemas Ward, Esq. (W. Dec. 26, '92.)

Brigham, Lucy, m. Capt. James Humphrey, jun.

Bright, John, last Thursday evening, at Braintree, Mr. J. B., of this town, to Miss Mary Adams, of that place. (S. Dec. 13, '88.)

Bright, Capt. Peter, in this town, by the Rev. Mr. Belknap, Capt. P. B., to Miss Nabby Balch. (S. May 7, '91.)

Bright, Polly, m. Thomas Adams.

Brightman, Mrs. Lucy, m. Beriah Havland.

Brimmer, Andrew, Mr. A. B., merchant, to Miss Polly Salmon, both of this town. (W. Feb. 20, '88.)

Brisco, Thomas, in this town, Mr. T. B., to Miss Sally Rose. (W. 23, '91.)

Bristor, Hon. Reuben, Hon. R. B., of New-Concord, to Miss Elizabeth Starkweather, of Preston. Bristow? (W. March 26, '94.)

Briton, James, at Staten-Island, J. B. Esq., to Miss Violetta Dissotway. (W. April 18, '92.)

Britton, Peggy, m. David C. Claypole.

Broadbrooks, John, in this town, Mr. J. B., to Miss Polly Atwood. (W. April 17, '93.)

Brooks, Miss, m. Francis Burns.

Brooks, Cotton Brown, at Salem, Mr. C. B. B., of Haverhill, to Miss Jane Williams. *(S. Dec. 20, '94.)

Brooks, Jonas, last Wednesday evening, Mr. J. B., of Lincoln, to Miss Rachel Greenough, of this town. (W. March 22, '86.)

Brooks, Mercy, m. Cotton Tufts, jun.

Brooks, Peter C., at Charlestown, Mr. P. C. B., to Miss Ann Gorham. (W. Nov. 28, '92.)

Brooks, Rebecca, m. Gerrit G. Vischer.

Brooks, Sally, m. Capt. Reuben Knight.

Brooks, William, Thursday evening, 12th inst., was celebrated the marriage of Mr. W. B., merchant in Exeter, and the amiable Miss Glover, second daughter of the Hon. John Glover, of Marblehead. (W. Oct. 18, '86.)

Brown, Miss, m. Robert Lewis.

Brown, Abby, m. John Francis.

Brown, Mrs. Abigail, m. Jonathan Freeman, jun.

Brown, Anna, m. William Proctor.

Brown, Benjamin, at Beverly, Mr. B. B., of Salem, to Miss Polly Pickard. (W. April 17, '93.)

Brown, Capt. Benjamin, at New-Haven, Capt. B. B., to Mrs. Rhoda Chatterton. (W. Oct. 31, '92.)

Brown, Betsy, m. John Hichborn.

Brown, Betsey, m. John M'Kinsey.

Brown, Ebenezer, at Roxbury, Mr. E. B., to Miss Katy Parker. (W. March 11, '89.)

Brown, Enoch, in this town, Mr. E. B., to Miss Betsy Barnard. (S. Dec. 1, '92.)

Brown, Enoch, on Thursday evening last, by the Rev. Mr. Elliot, Mr. E. B., to Miss Betsey Barnard, daughter to Capt. Thomas Barnard, of this town. (S. Dec. 22, '92.)

Brown, Francis, at Hartford, Mr. F. B., merchant, to Miss Polly Colt, of Lymes. (S. Oct. 18, '94.)

Brown, Hope, m. Thomas P. Ives.

Brown, Huldah, m. William Butler.

Brown, Capt. James, Capt. J. B., of this town, to Miss Hannah Watts, of Chelsea. (S. May 27, '86.)

Brown, John. Mr. J. B., to Miss Betsy Austin. (S. March 21, '89.)

Brown, Capt. John, at Cambridge, Capt. J. B., commander of the first troop of Cavalry, in the third division of the militia, to Mrs. Christine Phillips, both of that place. (W. Dec. 31, '94.)

Brown, Joseph, at Lynnfield, Mr. J. B., to Miss Sally Holt. (S. April 27, '93.)

Brown, Joseph, at Andover, Mr. J. B., of Tewksbury, to Miss Sally Foster, of the former place. (S. June 14, '94.)

Brown, Joseph, at Newbury-Port, Mr. J. B., to Miss Sally Nowell, of Amesbury. See also Sept. 20. (W. Sept. 10. '94.)

Brown, Joseph, at Newbury-Port, Mr. J. B., to Miss Sally Newell, of Amesbury. (S. Sept. 20, 1794).

Brown, Lydia M., William Manning.

Brown, Lydia, m. Capt. Nathaniel Marston.

Brown, Martha, m. Dr. Jeremiah B. Howell.

Brown, Moses, Mr. M. B., of Newbury-Port, merchant, to Miss Mary White, daughter of Samuel White, Esq., of Haverhill. (W. Oct. 11, '86.)

Brown, Nabby, m. John Graham.

Brown, Nancy, m. Samuel Masury.

Brown, Nicholas, at Newton, the 9th instant, N. B. Esq., of Providence, to Miss Avis Binney, eldest daughter of the late Capt. Binney, of this town. (W. Sept. 14, 1785.)

Brown, Nicholas, at Providence, N. B., Esq., merchant, to the aimable Miss Ann Carter, daughter of John Carter, Esq. (W. Nov. 16, 1791.)

Brown, Patty, m. Asa Hatch.

Brown, Polly, m. Joseph Callender, jun.

Brown, Sally, m. Henry Swift.

Brown, William, Mr. W. B., of this town, merchant, to Miss Betsy Livermore, daughter to the Hon. Judge Livermore, of Holderness, in New-Hampshire, and one of the Representatives of that State in Congress. (S. Nov. 20, 1790.)

Brown, Capt. William, at Newburyport, Capt. W. B., to Miss Katharine Jones. (S. April 6, 1793.)

Browne, Rev. John, at Cohasset, the Rev. J. B., pastor of the church in that place, to Mrs. Honour Fitzgerald, of this town. (W. Oct. 22, 1788.)

Brownell, Luther, at Westford, Mr. L. B., to Miss Elizabeth Dyer. (S. Jan. 11, 1794.)

Bruce, Stephen, on Sunday evening last, Mr. S. B., to Miss Rebecca Blake. (S. May 5, 1792.)

Bruce, William, [at New-York] Mr. W. B., to Miss Peggy Allen. (S. June 23, 1792.)

Bryant, Mrs., m. Daniel Wild.

Bryant, Betsy, m. Lt. Ebenezer Durton.

Bryant, Daniel, at Bridgewater, Mr. D. B., to Miss Jennet Mitchel. (S. Oct. 10, 1789.)

Bryant, Gamaliel, jun., at New-Bedford, Mr. G. B., jun., to Miss Polly Potter, both of that place. (W. Nov. 26, 1794.)

Bryant, James, in this town, Mr. J. B., to Miss Hannah Bumstead. (W. Oct. 24, 1792.)

Bryant, Perez, [in this town] Mr. P. B., to Miss Fanny Clark. (S. June 14, 1794.)

Buchman, Betsy, m. Jacob Thompson, jun.

Buck, Elizabeth, m. Joel Green.

Buckley, Betsy, m. Richard Conning.

Bucklin, Betsey, m. Samuel Edey.

Buckminster, Isabel, m. Amos Tappan.

Buckminster, Capt. Thomas, at Framingham, Capt. T. B., to Miss Keziah Bacon. (S. Feb. 8, 1794.)

Bull, Levina, m. Elias Morgan.

Buel, Ozias, at Litchfield, Conn., Mr. O. B., merchant of Kent, to Miss Nabby Catlin. (S. Feb. 18, 1792.)

Bugbee, Mrs. m. Capt. Allbee.

Bulfinch, Miss, m. Joshua Emmons.

Bulfinch, Charles, Mr. C. B., to Miss Hannah Apthorp. (W. Dec. 3, 1788.)

Married 20 November, architect of the Capital, Washington.

Bull, Lydia m. John Royse.

Bulfinch, Jeremiah, at Salem, Mr. J. B., of this town, to Mrs. Rebecca Cheever, of Salem. (W. Aug. 25, 1887.)

Bullock, Capt. William, at Barrington, Capt. W. B., to Miss Rebecca Allen. (W. Aug. 22, 1792.)

Bumstead, Abigail, m. T. H. Kemble.

Bumstead, Hannah, m. James Bryant.

Bumstead, Josiah, at Dedham, Mr. J. B., of this town, to Miss Abigail Baker, of Dedham. (S. Aug. 16, 1794.)

Bruce, Matthew, at New-York, Mr. M. B., to Miss Rebecca Smith, (S. Feb. 2, 1793.)

Burbeck, Capt. Henry, Capt. H. B., to Miss Abigail Webb, both of town. (W. March 17, 1790.)

Burbeck, Thomas, Mr. T. B., to Miss Sally Coverly, both of this town. (W. Oct. 17, 1787.)

Burchmore, Polly, m. Capt. John Foster.

Burgiss, Dea. Jacob, at Lanesborough, in this State, Dea. J. B., aged 81, to Mrs. Eiizabeth Weed, aged 63. See also Jared King. (S. Nov. 23, 1793.)

Burley, William, at Ipswich, Mr. W. B., of this town, to Miss Susannah Farley, daughter of the Hon. Michael Farley, Esq. (W. Dec. (23, 1786.)

Burneston, Isaac, at Baltimore, Mr. I. B., merchant, to Miss Ann Rutter, both of that place. (W. Feb. 8, 1792.)

Burvet, Benjamin, on Thursday evening last, Mr. B. B., to Miss Nancy Simpson. (S. Nov. 28, 1789.)

Burns, Francis, at Medford, Mr. T. B., to the amiable Miss Brooks, sister to the hon. major-general Brooks. (W. Oct. 22, 1794.)

Burr, Abigail, m. W. H. Capers.

Burr, Eunice D., m. B. Hedge, jun.

Burr, Gershom, [at Fairhaven] Mr. G. B., to Miss Young. See B. Hedge, jun. (W. Sept. 16, 1789.)

Burr, Rev. Jonathan, the Rev. J. B., of Sandwich, to Miss Sally Cooke, daughter of the late Rev. Mr. Samuel Cooke, of Cambridge. (W. Aug. 1, 1787.)

Burr, Susannah, m. Russell White.

Burr, Timothy, at New York, Mr. T. B., merchant, of Hartford, to Miss Maria Hurten, of New York. (Sept. 21, 1793.)

Burroughs, Amy Whipple, m. Henry Charles Jones.

Burroughs, Capt. Ezekiel, [in this town] Capt. E. B., to Miss Sally Torrey. (W. Nov. 26, 1794.)

Burroughs, Rebecca, m. John Jones.

Burt, Sally, m. Nathaniel Patten.

Burt, Sylvia, m. Daniel Lombard, jun.

Burtwell, James, [at New-London] Mr. J. B., to Miss Lovey Rogers. (W. Jan. 30, 1793.)

Buskirk, Rachel, m. James Swords.

Bussy, M., at New-York, M. B., chancellor to the Consulate in that city, to Miss Mary Howard. (S. Sept. 20, 1794.)

Butler, Daniel Mr. D. B., of Northampton, merchant, to Miss Nancy Welsh, daughter of Mr. John Welsh, of this town. (W. March 5, 1794.)

Butler, Sukey, m. Joseph Curtis

Cabot, Mehitable, m. Joseph Rouse.

Cadwallader, Elizabeth, m. Archibald M'Call, jun.

Cadwallader, Maria, m. Samuel Ringgold.

Calder, Robert. Mr. R. C. of Charlestown, to Miss Anna Davis, of Dorchester. (S. Apr. 9, 1791.)

Caldwell, Sarah, m. Rev. Joseph Dana.

Call, Miss, m. Samuel Perkins.

Call, Martha, m. John Atwater.

Call, Polly, m. Howes Manning.

Call, Mrs. Sarah, m. Richard Chamberlain.

Callahan, Capt. Frederick William. At Newport, Capt. F. W. C., of Boston, to Miss Merebe Handy. (W. Oct. 1, 1794.)

Callender, Benjamin. Mr. B. C., to Miss Eunice Flanlin, both of this town. (S. Dec. 24, 1785.)

Callender, John. At Georgetown (City of Washington) J. C., Esq., Attorney at Law, of this town, to Miss Catherine Lawless Templeman, of that place. (S. Dec. 13, 1794.)

Callender, Joseph. Mr. J. C., Engraver, to Miss Elizabeth Laughton. (S. Aug. 1, 1789.)

Callender, Joseph, jun. Mr. J. C., jun., to Miss Polly Brown, both of Boston. (W. Sept. 28, 1785.)

Callender, Lydia, m. Josiah Bradlee.

Callender, William. In this town, Mr. W. C. to Miss Katy Nickals. (W. Jan. 1, 1794.)

Calley, Hannah, m. James Carter Singleton.

Camp, Phœbe, m. Rev. Calvin White.

Campbell, Betsey, m. John Loring.

Campbell, Dr. George W. At Philadelphia, Dr. G. W. C., to Miss Charlotte Craig. (S. Mch. 23, 1793.)

Campbell, Hermoine B., m. Dan. Taylor.

Campbell, John. [At New-York] Mr. J. C., to Miss Sally Guest. (S. Feb. 2, 1793.)

Campbell, Patrick, jun. At York (P.) Mr. P. C., jun., to Miss F. Stockton. (W. Feb. 29, 1792.)

Cannon, Sarah, m. John Douglas.

Capen, Polly, m. Jeremiah Fowle.

Capen, Stoddard. Mr. S. C., to Miss Margaret Jennings [both of this town]. (W. Apr. 9, 1794.)

Capers, W. H. [At Fairhaven] Mr. W. C., of S. Carolina, to Miss Abigail Burr. (W. Sept. 16, 1789.) See B. Heoge, jun.

Capper, Henry. At Philadelphia, Mr. H. C., to Miss Bartholomew. (S. Apr. 14, 1792.)

Carey, Matthew. At Philadelphia, Mr. H. C., printer, to Miss Flahaven.

Carey, Rachel, m. Samuel Thayer.

Carey, Sukey, m. John Trueman.

Carnes, John, jun. Mr. J. C., jun., to Miss Nabby Wainwright. (S. Sept. 9, 1786.

Carnes, Capt. Lewis. Capt. L. C., to Miss Martha Green, daughter to the late Nathaniel Green, Esq. (W. Feb. 16, 1791.)

Carnes, Thomas. Last Sunday evening. Mr. T. C., to Miss Polly Davis, daughter of Mr. William Davis, of this town, merchant. (W. July 9, 1788.)

Carney, Daniel. By the Rev. Dr. Stillman, Mr. D. C., to the amiable Miss Sally Bell, both of this town. (W. Mch. 21, 1792.)

Carr, Capt. John. At Newport, Capt. J. C., to Mrs. Northup. (S. Nov. 19, 1791.)

Carrington, Hon. Paul. In Virginia, the Hon. P. C., Judge of the High Court of Appeals, in the 65th year of his age, to Miss Simms, of Halifax County, aged 15. (W. Apr. 25, 1792.)

Carpenter, Elizabeth, m. Thomas Lewis.

Carr, Jane, m. John Bartlétt.

Carr, Mrs. Rebecca, m. James Murray.

Carter, Ann, m. Nicholas Brown.

Carter, Ann, m. Gov. Lee.

Carter, Bartholemew. In this town, Mr. B. C., to the amiable Miss Eliza Appleton, both of this town. (W. Mch. 28, 1792.)

Carter, Hannah, m. William Smith.

Carter, James, at Haverhill, Mr. J. C., merchant, of Newbury-port, to Mrs. Elizabeth Thaxter, of Haverhill. (S. Sept. 6, 1794.)

Carter, Nathaniel, jun. Mr. N. C. jun., of Newbury-Port, to Miss Cutts, of Portsmouth. (W. May 14, 1788.)

Carter, Timothy. At Concord (N. H.), Mr. T. C., to Miss Judith Chandler. (S. June 28, 1794.)

Cartmill, Mary, m. Nathaniel Willis.

Carver, Miss, m. Dr. Samuel Angier.

Cary, Edward, jun. At Charlestown, Mr. E. C., jun. of Nantucket, to the amiable Miss Russell. (W. Oct. 2, 1793.)

Cary, Samuel. On Sunday last, Mr. S. C., to Miss Susannah Coverly, both of this town. (W. Mch. 5, 1794.)

Carhcart, John. Last evening by the Rev. Mr. Eliot, J. C., Esq., to Miss Polly B. Sigourney, of this town. (W. Dec. 29, 1790.)

Catlin, Nabby, m. Ozias Buel.

Cay, Mrs., m. Jeremiah Finney.

Cazneau, Hannah, m. Thomas Brewer.

Cazneau, Isaac. At Andover, Mr. I. C., to Miss Anna Symer, daughter to the Rev. William Symer, of that place. (S. Dec. 7, 1793.)

Cazneau, Rebecca, m. William Alline.

Chadbourne, Jonathan. J. C., Esq., of Berwick, to Miss Nancy Hale, of Portsmouth, daughter of Samuel Hale, Esq. (W. Mch. 3, 1790.)

Chadwick, Hannah, m. Capt. Joseph Clasby.

Chadwick, Hezekiah. Mr. H. C., to Miss Hannah Voax. (S. Mch. 20, 1790.)

Chaloner, John. At Springfield, Mr. J. C., to Miss Experience Bliss,—This is the same Mr. Chaloner, who lost both his arms, by the discharge of a field-piece on Federal Hill, during the Insurrection. We sincerely hope, although married to an invalid, the above lady will through life, consummate her maiden names. (W. Mch. 7, 1792.) Deaths: At Springfield, Mr. William Chaloner, Æt. 45. He was the unfortunate person who had both his arms blown from his body by the discharge of a cannon. (But W. July 10, 1793, called William.)

Chamberlain, Richard. In this town, by the Rev. Mr. Belknap, Mr. R. C., to Mrs. Sarah Call. (W. Dec. 5, 1792.)

Champlin, Elizabeth, m. John Coffin Jones.

Champney, Hannah, m. James Prescott, jun.

Champney, Richard. At Portsmouth (N. H.), R. C., Esq., to Mrs. Betsy Hickey. (W. Mch. 3, 1790.)

Chandler, Abner. At Springfield (Mass.), Mr. A. C., to Miss Eunice Colton. (S. Oct. 27, 1792).

Chandler, Eliza Augusta, m. Francis Blake.

Chandler, Elizabeth, m. Nathaniel Paine.

Chandler, Judith, m. Timothy Carter.

Chandler, Lucretia, m. Rev. Aaron Bancroft.

Chandler, Mrs. Nancy, m. William Chandler.

Chandler, William. On Thursday evening, Mr. W. C., to Mrs. Nancy Chandler, both of this town. (S. Aug. 13, 1791.)

Channing, Nancy, m. William Woodbridge.

Chapman, Capt. Jonathan. Capt. J. C., to Miss Nabby Devans, daughter of Richard Devans, Esq. (S. Sept. 10, 1785.)

Chapman, Joseph, at Marblehead, Mr. J. C., to Miss Susannah Lee, both of that place. (W. Sept. 3, 1794.)

Chapman, Sally, m. John Bray.

Chappertin, Lem. [In this town] Mr. L. C., to Miss Bridget Coleman, daughter of Col. Coleman, of this town. (S. July 19, 1794.)

Chatterton, Mrs. Rhoda, m. Capt. Benjamin Brown.

Chauncey, Johanna, m. Edward Parry.

Checkley, Nancy, m. Rev. William Shaw.

Cheever, Dr. Abijah. Last Sunday noon, Dr. A. C., to Miss Betsey Scott—Mr. Samuel Cobb to Miss Peggy Scott, daughters of the late Dr. Samuel Scott. (W. July 8, 1789.)

Cheever, Jemima, m. Daniel Hawes.

Cheever, Rebecca, m. Jeremiah Bullfinch.

Chicken, John. J. C. Esq., aged 61, to Mrs. Lackay, aged 77 years, both of Kent's County, Delaware. (S. June 9, 1792.)

Childs, Miss, m. Dea. Wells.

Childs, Amariah. At Charlestown, Mr. A. C., merchant, to Miss Ruthy Larkin, daughter of Mr. Ebenezer Larkin, of that town. (S. May 12, 1792.

Childs, Francis. At Elizabeth-Town, New Jersey, Mr. F. C., editor of the New-York Daily Advertiser, to Miss Sarah Blanchard, daughter of Mr. John Blanchard, merchant, of Elizabeth-Town. (M. Aug, 13, 1787.)
Boston Gazette.

Chinery, Anna, m. Mr. Aspinwall.

Chipman, Paulina, m. Michael Morrison.

Chipman, Rev. Thomas Henley. On Thursday evening, by the Rev. Mr. Stillman, the Rev. T. H. C., of Annapolis-Royal, to Miss Jave Harding, daughter of the late deceased Capt. Thomas Harding, of Charlestown. (S. Oct. 28, 1786.)

Chittendon, Ruthy, m. Joseph Bond.

Choate, Nancy, m. James Tappan.

Chollet, John B. In this town, Mr. J. B. C., to Mrs. Mary Danet. (W. Feb. 20, 1793.)

Coarley, Capt. John Willson. In this town, on Thursday evening, by the Rev. Dr. Parker, Capt. J. W. C., to Miss Theodosia Beale. (S. June 2, 1792.)

Christopher, Peter. At New London, Mr. P. C. to Miss Rebecca Sultonstall [Saltonstall?] (S. Apr. 14, 1792.)

Church, Abigial, m. Thomas Foord.

Church, Nancy, m. Thomas Dickman.

Churchill, Ansell. At Warren, Mr. A. C., to Miss Lillis Barton, daughter of William Barton, Esq. of that town. (S. Mch. 31, 1792.)

Churchill, Francis. At Charlestown, by the Rev. President Willard, Mr. F. C, to Miss Phœbe Leathers. (S. Sept. 30, 1786.)

Churchman, Enoch. In Hartford County, (M.) Mr. E. C., merchant, to Miss Patty Norris. (W. Feb. 29, 1792.)

Clap, Levy. [In this town] Mr. L. C., to Miss Elizabeth Wallace. (W. Apr, 23, 1794.)

Clap, Samuel, On Thursday evening, Mr. S. C., to Miss Deziah Lamb, [both of this town]. (S. Oct. 23, 1790.)

Clap, William T. In this town, Mr. W. T. C., to Miss Lucretia Hewes. (W. Apr., 23, 1794.)

Clapp, A. At Dorchester, Mr. A. C., of Northampton, to Miss Esther Tileston, of that place. (W. Apr. 12, 1794.)

Clapp, Abigail, m. Hawke Cushing.

Clapp, Caleb. In this town, Mr. C. C., to Miss Nancy Dorr. (W. Apr. 24, 1793.)

Clapp, John. At Dorchester, Mr. J. C., of Roxbury, to Miss Sukey Robbins, of Dorchester. (S. Nov. 24, 1794.)

Clapp, Capt. Joshua. At Deerfield, Capt. Joshua Clapp, of Burlington, (Vt.) to Miss Abigial Barnard, of that town: Mr. Hart Leavit, of Greenfield, to Miss Rachel Barnard: Dr. Stone, of Greenfield, to Miss Sally Barnard. It may be worthy to remark, that the *brides* were all *sisters*, and *one* matrimonial eve made *wives* of the whole. (S. Feb. 16, 1793.)

Clapp, Capt. Samuel, Capt. S. C., to Miss Esther Coit. (S. Mch. 31 1792.) "At Connecticut" implied.

Clarke, Betsy, m. Rufus Sweet.

Clark, Elinora, m. Dudley Walker.

Clark, Fanny, m. Perez Bryant.

Clark, Gregory. At Dorchester, Mr. G. C., of this town, to Miss Lucy Vose, of that place. (W. Apr., 1789.)

Clark, Hitty, m. Capt. John Round.

Clark, James. In London, J. C. Esq., to Miss Margaret Lee, youngest daughter to the late Hon. Philip Thomas Lee. (W. Mch. 13, 1793.)

Clark, Capt. Joseph. On Thursday last, Capt. J. C., to Miss Judith Howard, "May she love him, and may he her behold, advanced in years but never think her old." (W. Mar. 23, 1785.)

Clark, Mary, m. Stephen Farrond.

Clark, Nabby, m. Isaac Larkin.

Clark, Patty, m. Rev. William Harris.

Clark, Patty, m. John Molly.

Clark, Sally, m. Philip Currell.

Clark, Sally, m. Remember Preston, junr.

Clark, Thomas P. At Providence, Mr. T. P. C., to Miss Ruth Dunton. (W. May 21, 1794,)

Clarke, Eben. Mr. E. C., to Miss Katy Coffin. (S. Dec. 7, 1793.) At Nantucket?

Clarke, John. In this town, Mr. J. C., Coppersmith, to Miss Sally Davis. (S. Oct. 16, 1790.)

Clarke, Mrs. Martha, m. Rev. James Freeman.

Clarkson, Gen. Matthew. At New-York, Gen. M. C., to Miss Sally Cornell, (W. Feb. 29, 1792.)

Clasby, Capt. Joseph. [At Nantucket] Capt. J. C., to Miss Hannah Chadwick. (S. Dec. 15, 1782,)

Clay, Polly, m. Capt. William Wilson.

Clayhole, David C. At Philadelphia, Mr. D. C. C., Printer, to Miss Peggy Britton, daughter of Thomas Britton, Esq. (W. Oct. 26, 1791.)

Clear, Mrs. Sally, m. John Thomas.

Cleland, William. Last Thursday evening, Mr. W. C., to Miss Elizabeth Iven, daughter of the late Treasurer of this Commonwealth. (S. Nov. 13, 1790.)

Clements, Charles. On Thursday evening last, Mr. C. C., to Miss Lydia Rich. (S. May 5, 1792.)

Cheney, Mrs. Sally, m. Daniel Mason.

Clinton, Cordelia, m. M. Ganet.

Clipton, Caleb. [In this town] Mr. C. C., to Miss Sarah Barton. (S. Nov. 29, 1794.)

Clough, Ebenezer. Last evening, Mr. E. C., to the amiable Miss Catherine F. Bradbury, both of this town. (W. June 29, 1791.)

Clouston, William. Mr. W. C., to Miss Sally White. (S. Nov. 24, 1787.)

Cloutman, Hannah, m. Thomas Vincent.

Clulow, Elizabeth, m. John Thompson.

Clymer, Margaret, m. George McCall.

Coates, Deborah, m. Samuel Maynard.

Coates, John. At Marlborough, last Sunbay morning, Mr. S. C., of this town, to Miss Maria Howe, of that place. (S. May 17. 1794.)

Coates, Lydia, m. Capt. Benjamin S. Williams.

Cobb, Betsey, m. A le Smith.

Cobb, Eunice, m, Samuel Sumner Wilde.

Cobb, Nathaniel. Mr. N. C., of Leicester, to Miss Anne Knap, of Spencer. (W. May 2, 1792.) At New York perhaps implied.

Cobb, Samuel. [Last Sunday noon] Mr. S. C., to Miss Peggy Scott. (W. July 8, 1789.) See Dr. Abijah Cheever.

Cochran, Alexander. Mr. A. C., mer., to Miss Phebe Meeker. (W. Mch. 14, 1792.)

Cockey, Penelope Deye, m. Col. Thomas Gist.

Codman, Capt. James. [At Portland] Capt. J. C., to Miss Betsey Waite. (S. Nov. 5, 1791.)

Codman, John, jun. On Monday evening, by the Rev. Dr. Parker, J. C., jun., Esq., to Miss Catherine Amory, a lady of great merit. (W. Feb. 16, 1791.)

Codman, Capt. Richard. At Portland, Capt. R. C., to Miss Statira Preble. (W. Sept. 16, 1789.)

Codman, Capt. William. At Portland, Capt. W. C., of this town, to Miss Suskey Coffin, of Portland. (S. Nov. 5, 1791.)

Coe, Rev. James. At New York, Rev. J. C., to Miss Betsy Miller. (S. Oct. 18, 1794.)

Coffin, Anne, m. Dr. Oliver Smith.

Coffin, Charles. At Nantucket, Mr. C. C., to Mrs. Meriam Parker. (S. Dec. 15, 1792.)

Coffin, Ebenezer. At Newburyport, Mr. E. C., to Miss Mary Newell. (W. Oct. 23, 1793.)

Coffin, Katy, m. Eber Clarke.

Coffin, Mary, m. Dr. Peter Easton.

Coffin, Polly Foster, m. Ebenezer Mayo.

Coffin, Polly, m. Jonathan Colesworthy.

Coffin, Suskey, m. Capt. William Codman.

Cogswell, Nabby, m. Daniel Lillie, jun.

Cogswell, William. At Ipswich, Mr. W. C., to Mrs. Hannah Lamson, of Ammas. (S. June, 1794.)

Coit, Easter, m. Capt. Samuel Clapp.

Coit, Capt. Elisha. At New London, Capt. E. C., merchant, of New York, to Miss Rebecca Manwaring, of New London. (W. Jan. 30, 1793).

Coit, Wheeler, [At Norwich] Mr. W. C., to Miss Hannah Abell (S. Nov. 23, 1793).

Colden, Catherine, m. Thomas Cooper.

Cole, Edward. In this town, Mr. E.C., to Miss Nancy Farnam. (W. June 30, 1790.)

Colesworthy, Jonathan Waldo. [At Nantucket] Mr. J. W. C., to Miss Polly Coffin. (S. Dec. 15, 1792.)

Colleswortby, Nancy, m. Lot Hayden.

Collins, Miss, m. Richard Bland Lee.

Collings, Mr. In this town, last evening, by the Rev. Mr. Baldwin, Mr. C., to Mrs. Whitfield, both of the Boston Theatre. (S. Jan. 25, 1794.)

On S. Mch. 8, 1794, "Spectater" wrote, "Mr. Collins grows upon the audience, and every performance adds to his popularity." and of Mrs. Collins, "The extre diffidence Mrs. Collins is an obstruction to her performance and commands our tenderness." W. May 28, 1794, "A card to the canded public," signed Richard Collins, is of some interest.

Collins, Hannah, m. Josiah Flagg, jr.

Collins, Isabella, m. Daniel Jennings.

Collins, Mrs. Lydia, m. William Ellis.

Colman, Bridget, m. Leon Chappertin.

Colman, Samuel. At Norfolk, (Virginia) Mr. S. C., Deputy Collector of that port, to Miss Saily Marlean. (W. Dec. 11, 1793.)

Colt, Polly, m. Francis Brown.

Colton, Eunice, m. Abner Chandler.

Coman, Mrs. Sabra, m. Gen. Towne.

Comstock, Lydia, m. Lewis Dexter.

Conant, Major Jeremiah. At Bridgewater, Mr. J. C., of Pomfret (Vt.), to Miss Cloe Prati, of that town, (Cloe Pratt?). (S. Feb. 8, 1794).

Conant, Silence, m. Appleton Prentiss.

Condy, Capt. Thomas Hollis. At Patuxet, Capt. T. H. C., of this town, to the amiable Miss Polly Aborn, of that place. (W. June 17, 1789).

Conner, Peggy, m. Daniel Finaly Flynn.

Conning, Richard. In this town, Mr. R. C., to Miss Betsey Buckley. (S. June 30, 1792.)

Cook, Sally, m. Stephen Swift.

Cook, Silas. At Newark (N. J.) Mr. S. C., to Miss Morrison. (W. Feb. 29, 1792.)

Cook, Wm. [At Newburyport], Mr. W. C., to Miss Catherine Poor. (S. Nov. 1, 1794.)

Cooke, Sally, m. Rev. Jonathan Burr.

Cookson, Major. Major C., to Mrs. Osborne [both of this town]. (S. Oct. 5, 1793.)

Cooledge, Hepsey, m. Henry Ayres.

Cooldridge, William. In this town, Mr. W. C., merchant, to Miss Maria May, daughter of Mr. Aaron May. (W. Dec. 1, 1790.)

Coombs, Ebenezer. In this town, Mr. E. C., to Miss Peggy Hunter, (S. Sept. 27, 1794.)

Cooper, Elizabeth, m. Joseph Wittemore.

Cooper, Jacob. At New-London, Mr. J. C., of West-Springfield, Miss Rebecca Spooner. (S. Oct. 3, 1792.)

Cooper, John. Last Thursday evening, by the Rev. Mr. Thatcher, J. C., Esq. of Machias, to Miss Elizabeth Savage, of this town. S. June 25, 1791)

Cooper, Richard W. At Petersburg, (Virginia), on Tuesday, 18th December, by the Rev. Mr. Cameron, Mr. R. W. C, to the amiable Miss Priscilla Inglish, both of this town. (W. Jan. 23, 1788.)

Cooper, Samuel. Mr. S. C., to Miss Peggy Phillips, both of this town. (S. Dec. 10, 1785.)

Cooper, Thomas. At New-York, T. C., Esq., to Miss Catherine Colden. (S. April 21, 1792.)

Copeland, Ephraim. Last week, Mr. E. C., to Miss Bethiah Baker, youngest daughter of the late Mr. William Baker. (S. Nov. 29, 1788.)

Copeland, Josiah. Mr. J. C., to Miss Polly Holman, both of this town. (S. Aug. 19, 1786.)

Copeland, Nathaniel. Mr. N. C., to Miss Polly Page, [both] of this town. (W. Nov. 17, 1790.)

Corbet, David. [In this town] Mr. D. C., to Miss Deborah Cowing. (S. Dec. 8, 1792.)
Corbet, Nancy, m. William Frobisher.
Corbet, Rebecca, m. John Francis.
Cordis, Rebecca, m. John Wallay Langdon.
Cordwell, William. Mr. W. C., to Miss Sally Greenough. (W. Nov. 29, 1786.)
Corey, Benjamin. At Roxbury, Mr. B. C., to Miss Betsy Ward. (S. Feb. 7, 1789.)
Corey, Dame. [at Westport] Mr. D. C., to Miss Rebecca Earl. (S. Jan. 11, 1794.)
Cornell, Hannah, m. Herman Leroy.
Cornell, Sally, m. General Matthew Clarkson.
Cornet, Madame de, m. J. J. Madey.
Cornette, Mariette, m. John Cormerais Del'horme.
Coskery, Patty, m. Charles O'Brien.
Cotten, Lucy, m. Charles Jackson.
Cotting, Dr. Josiah. At Lancaster, Dr. J. C., of Southborough, to Miss Maverick Houghton, of Lancaster. (W. March 14, 1792.)
Cotton, Andrew. At Springfield, Mr. A. .C, to Mrs. Lydia White. (S. Oct. 9, 1790.)
Cotton, Elizabeth, m. John Hinds.
Cotton, John. Mr. J. C., painter, to Miss Sukey Davies, daughter of Mr. Nathan Davies.
Cotton, Sally, m. Martin Siders.
Cousins, Nancy, m. Gubbins Osborn.
Coverly, Mary Dwight, m. Nathaniel H. Richardson.
Coverly, Sally, m. Thomas Burbeck.
Coverly, Samuel. Last evening, Mr. S. C., merchant, to Miss Sally Winslow, both of this town. (W. Nov. 28, 1787.)
Coverly, Susannah, m. Samuel Cary.
Cowden, Daniel. In this town, Mr. D. C., merchant to Miss Zebiah Davis, daughter of Amasa Davis, Esq. (W. Oct. 16, 1793.)
Cowdin, Capt. Joseph. At Fitchburg, Capt. J. C., merchant, of this town, to Miss Maria Fox, of that place. (W. Dec. 28, 1799.)
Cowell, Abigail, m. Capt. John Davison.
Cowell, Capt. William, jun. [In this town] Capt. W. C., jun., to an agreeable young lady. (S. Sept. 20, 1794.)

Cowing, Deborah, m. David Corbet.
Cowing, Fanny, m. John Adams.
Cox, Capt. Gersham. At Hallowell, Capt. G. C., to Miss Sally Hussey. (W. Dec., 31, 1794.)
Cox, Hannah, m. Jesse Kimball.
Cox, Mary, m. Richard Skillings.
Cox, Polly, m. Timothy Goodwin.
Cox, Susanne, m. Simon Tufts.
Crafts, Fanny, Jonathan D. Robins.
Crafts, Foster. [In this town] Mr. F. C., to Miss Hannah Hinkley. (S. Nov. 24, 1792.)
Crafts, Nancy, m. John Halsey.
Crafts, Percis, m. John Doan.
Craig, Charlotte, m. Dr. George W. Campbell.
Craigie, Andrew. On Tuesday evening, Mr. A. C., of Cambridge, to Miss Betsy Shaw, of Nantucket. (S. Jan. 12, 1793.)
Cranch, Betsy, m. Rev. Jacob Norton.
Cranden, Philip. At New-Bedford, Mr. P. C., to Miss Esther Dillingham. (S. Dec. 7, 1793.)
Crane, Mehitable, m. James Barry.
Crane, Stephen. In this town, last evening, by the Rev. Mr. Belknap, Mr. S. C., of Watertown, to Miss Betsey Gardiner, of this town. (W. Nov. 2, 1791.)
Crave, Thomas. Mr. T. C., to Mrs. Pease. (S. April 4, 1789.)
Crave, Ziba. Mr. Z. C., to Mrs. Abigail Pratt. (S. Apr. 2, 1791.)
Creese, John. In this town, Mr. J. C., to Miss Rachel McLintock. (S. June 18, 1791.)
Creese, Samuel. Mr. S. C., to Miss Betsey Warden. (W. Apr. 10, 1788.)
Crocker, Mrs. Deborah, m. Benjamin Gorham.
Crocker, Doddridge. Mr. D. C., to Miss Betsy Hichborn, daughter to Mr. Thomas Hichborn, of this town. (S. Sept. 18, 1790.)
Crocker, Robert. Mr. R. C., to Miss Polly Howe, [both of this town]. (S. Nov. 27, 1790.)
Crocket, Mrs. Sarah, m. Simon Wilmer.
Crombie, Nancy, m. Mr. Dunbar.
Crombie, William, jun. At Plymouth, Mr. W. C., jun., to Miss Nabby Jackson. (S. July 19, 1794.)

Crone, Sally, m. John Pray.
Crosby, Eunice, m. Henry Payson.
Crosby, James. In this town, Mr. J. C., to Mrs. Harriet Read. (W. April 3, 1793.)
Crosby, John. At Ashby, Mr. J. C., of New-Ipswich, to the amiable Miss Hitty Locke, of that place. (W. Nov. 13, 1793.)
Cross, Joseph. On Tuesday evening last, Mr. J. C., of this town, to Mrs. Sally Edson, of Taunton. (S. Sept. 15, 1792.)
Crossing, Mrs., m. Parker Hall.
Cummenes, William. At Roxbury, Mr. W. C., to Miss Polty Mayo. (W. March 13, 1793.)
Cunnabell, Eunice, m. Dr. Simeon Stevens.
Cunningham, Nathaniel F. At Lurenburg, on Thursday evening last, Mr. N. F. C., to the aimable Miss Nancy Adams, second daughter of the Rev. Zabdiel Adams, of that place. (W. Nov. 9, 1791.)
Cunningham, William, jun. In this town, Mr. W. C., jun., merchant, to Miss Lois May, both of Boston. (W. March 3, 1790.)
Currell, Philip. [In this town] Mr. P. C., to Miss Sally Clark. (W July 16, 1794.)
Curtis, Edward. Mr. E. C., to Miss Polly Marshall, both of this town. (S. Aug. 4, 1787.)
Curtis, Joseph. Mr. J. C., to the amiable Miss Sukey Butler. (W. April 9, 1794.)
Curtis, Lydia, m. P. C. Waterbury.
Curtis, Thomas. Mr. T. C., of this town, distiller, to Miss Helena Pelham, of Newton. (S. Jan. 8, 1791.)
Curtiss, Mrs. Betsey, m. Elisha Tichenor.
Curtiss, Edward. At Braintree, last evening, by the Rev. Mr. Wibutt, Mr. E. C., to Miss Hannah Wise. (W. Sept. 2, 1789.)
Cushing, Edward. Mr. E. C., to Miss Mary Goodale, [both] of this town. (S. June 7, 1794; repeated W. June 11.)
Cushing, Elizabeth, m. Capt. John Jencker.
Cushing, Hannah, m. Samuel Neatt.
Cushing, Hawke. At Hingham, Mr. H. C., to Miss Abigail Clapp. (W. Nov. 28, 1792.)
Cushing, Col. Job. At Shrewsbury, Col. J. C., to Mrs. Goulding. (S. June 16, 1792.)
Cushing, Katy, m. Samuel Andrews.

Cushing, Martin. (At Bath, Kennebeck) Mr. M. C., to Miss Hannah Sewall. (W. Nov. 12, 1794.)

Cushing, Sally, m. Thomas Barry.

Cushing, Thomas C. At Brooklyn, Mr. T. C C., of Salem, printer, to the amiable Miss Sally Dean, daughter of Mr. John Dean, of Brooklyn. (S. March 5, 1791.)

Cushman, Jotham. At Pembrosce, Mr. J. C., Esq., Attorney at Law, to Miss Racheal Hobart. (W. Oct. 1, 1794.)

Under "marriage corrected" this is repeated letter for letter. (S. Oct. 4.)

Cutler, Benjamin C. At Hampsted Place, near George-Town, [S. C.] Mr. B C. C., merchant, of this town, to Mrs. S. Hyrne, of that state. (S. Feb. 15, 1794. W. Feb. 19, 1794.)

Cutler, James. In Salem, Mr. J. C., in the 73d year of his age, to Miss Huldah Symonds, in her 19th year. (W. May 19, 1787.)

Cutler, James. [In this town] Mr. J. C., to Miss Sullivan, daughter to the Hon. James Sullivan, Esq. (W. Dec 26, 1792.)

Cutler, James. In this town, Mr. J. C., to Miss Mehitable Sullivan, daughter to the Hon. James Sullivan, Esq. (S. Feb. 9, 1793.)

Be their's the more refin'd delights
Of love, that banishes control;
Where the fond heart with heart unites,
And soul's in unison with soul.

Cutler, Jane, m. Jeremiah Schuyler.

Cutler, Samuel. [At Newbury-Port] Mr S C., to Miss Lydia Prout. (W. Jan. 15, 1794.)

Cutler. Dr. William. In this town, Dr. W. C., of Weston, to Miss Betsy Henderson, daughter to Joseph Henderson, Esq , of this town. (S. July 23, 1790.)

Cutler, Gershom. Mr. G. C., to Miss Deborah Torrey. (W. March 18, 1789.)

Cutter, Polly, m. Samuel Turell.

Cutts, Miss, m. Nathaniel Carter, jun.

Dabney, John. At Salem, Mr. J. D., stationer, to Miss Abigail Mason Peale, daughter of Capt. Jonathan Peale. (W. June 30, 1790).

Dafforne, Mrs. Elizabeth, m. William Wedgery.

Dagget, Deliverance, m. William Robinson.

Dagget, Eunice, m. William Howes.
Dagget, Samuel, jun. Mr. S. D., jun., to Miss Rebecca Daggett. (W. Oct. 27, 1790.)
Daggett, Rebecca, m. Samuel Dagget, jun.
Daland, Benjamid, jun. At Beverly, Mr. B. D., jun., to Miss Hannah Foster. (W. Nov. 7, 1792.)
Dall, Elizabeth, m. Caleb Wheaton.
Dalton, Abigail, m. John W. Blanchard.
Dalton, Polly, m. Leonard White.
Dalton, Ruth H., m. Lewis Deblois.
Dalton, Sally, m. Dr. John Homans.
Dana, Frances Johnstone, m. Joseph Sherburne.
Dana, James. Mr. J. D., of Cambridge, to Miss Katy Greaton, daughter of the late General Greaton. (S. Sept. 4, 1790.)
Dana, Rev. Joseph. At Barre, the Rev. J. D., to the amiable Miss Sarah Caldwell. (S. Sept. 6, 1788.)
Danet, Mrs. Mary, m. John B. Chollet.
Danforth, Dr. Samuel. Dr. S. D., to Miss Patty Gray. (S. Dec. 6, 1788.)
Daniels, John. [At Portsmouth] Mr. J. D., to Miss Hannah Tuttle. (S. Sept. 20, 1794.)
Daniels, Polly, m. Joseph Harris.
Daniels, Sally, m. Pliny Heartshorn.
Darney, John B. At Dedham, Mr. J. B. D., merchant, of Alexandria, to Miss Roxa Lewis, of that place. (S. Nov. 3, 1792.)
Dart, Anna, m. John Ferry.
Dashwood, Nancy, m. Joseph Baxter.
Dashwood, Samuel. On Sunday evening, by the Rev. Dr. Lathrop, Mr. S. D., to Miss Sally Homer. (W. Aug. 24, 1785.)
Davenport, Sally, m. Stephen Bradley.
Davenport, Thomas. At Milton, Mr. T. D., to Miss Deborah Whitehead. (W. Dec. 5, 1792.)
Davidson, James. At Georgetown, J. D. Esq., of Bath, merchant, to Miss Polly Lithgow. (W. Jan. 8, 1794.)
Davies, Miss, m. Edward Sohier.
Davies, Sukey, m. John Cotton.
Davis, Anna, m. Robert Calder.
Davis, Charlotte, m. Joseph Fosdick.

Davis, Capt. Edward. In England, Capt. E. D., of this town, to Miss Outram, of Gravesend. (W. April 25, 1787.)
Davis, Elizabeth, m. Capt. William Bordman.
Davis, Elizabeth, m. John Underwood.
Davis, Frances, m. Capt. Samuel Prince.
Davis, Hannah, m. Benjamin Brackett.
Davis, John. At Plymouth, by the Rev. Chandler Robbins, Mr. J. D., Attorney at law, to the amiable Miss Ellen Watson, youngest daughter of William Watson, Esq. (W. June 21, 1786.)
Davis, John. At Concord, Mr. J. D., of New-Ipswich, to the accomplished Miss Grace Allen, of that town. (W. Nov. 13, 1793.)
Davis, John. [At Nantucket] Mr. J. D., to Miss Jemima Glover. (S. Dec. 14, 1793.)
Davis, Lucinda, m. William Dorr.
Davis, Lucy, m. William Hayden.
Davis, Mary, m. John Knapp, jun.
Davis, Matilda, m. Jeremiah Williams.
Davis, Polly, m. Elijah Russel.
Davis, Polly, m. Thomas Carnes.
Davis, Rebecca, m. Capt. Job Gorham.
Davis, Ruth, m. Thomas Gray.
Davis, Sally, m. John Clarke.
Davis, Sally, m. Capt. William Boardman.
Davis, Samuel. At Roxbury, by Rev. Mr. Bradford, Mr. S. D., to Miss Polly Wheaton, both of that place. (S. Dec. 13, 1794.)
Davis, Zebiah, m. David Cowden.
Davison, Capt. John. On Tuesday evening last, Capt. J. D., to Miss Abigail Cowell. (S. May 5, 1792.)
Dawes, Elizabeth, m. Theodore French.
Dawes, Isabella, m. Obediah Whiston.
Dawes, Reuben. Mr. R. D., to Miss Polly Bentley. (S. Nov. 20, 1790.)
Dawes, Sally, m. Asa Hammond.
Day, Lydia, m. Henry Dwight.
Day, Matthias. At Newark, Mr. M. D., to Miss Hannah Ward. (W. March 6, 1793.)
Dayton, Col. Ebenezer. [At Newport] Col. E. D., to Mrs. Mary Goddard. (W. Oct. 1, 1794.)

Dean, Bethiah, m. Joshua Pope.
Dean, Polly, m. Ephraim Raymond.
Dean, Polly, m. Jared King.
Dean, Sally, m. Thomas C. Cushing.
Dearborn, Joseph. At Portsmouth, Mr. J. D., of N. Hill, to Miss Sally Seavey. (S. Nov. 22, 1794.)
Dearborn, Nabby, m. Rev. John Kelly.
Dearing, Hannah, m. Samuel Leavitt.
Dearing, Lucy, m. Dr. Robert Rogerson.
Deblois, Lewis. At Newbury-Port, Mr. L. D., merchant, to Miss Ruth H. Dalton, eldest daughter to the Most Hon. Tristram Dalton, Esquire. (S. July 25, 1789.)
Deblois, Stephen. In this town. Mr. S. D., merchant, of Portland, to Miss Elizabeth Amory, second daughter of the late Mr. Thomas Amory, of this town. (W. Sept. 26, 1792.)
Deblois, William. At Salem, on Saturday last, Mr. W. D., of this town, to Miss Sally Williams, daughter of Captain Samuel Williams, of Salem. (W. Oct. 12, 1785.)
Delano, Ebenezer. At Duxbury, Mr. E. D., aged nearly 80, to Miss Lydia Tower, aged 38 years. (W. Nov. 26, 1794.)
Delano, Sally, m. Beriah Fitch.
Delano, William. At New-Bedford, Mr. W. D., to Miss Hannah Tallman. (S. Jan. 11, 1794.)
Del'horme, John Cormerais. At Guadaloupe, Mr. J. C. D., merchant, of this place, to Miss Mariette Cornette. (W. Jan. 20, 1790.)
Dennis, Samuel. [At Newburyport] Mr. S. D., to Miss Elizabeth Pillsbury. (S. Nov. 1, 1794.)
Derby, Ezekiel Hersy. At Salem, Mr. E. H. D., to Miss Hannah Brown Fitch, daughter of the late Timothy Fitch, Esq., of Medford. (W. Sept. 24, 1794.)
Derby, Capt. John. Capt. J. D., of Salem, to Mrs. Elizabeth Pierce, of this town. (W. Oct. 17, 1787.)
Derby, Capt. John. [At Salem] Capt. J. D. to Miss Sally Barton. (W. Nov. 30, 1791.)
Derby, Polly, m. Samuel Preble.
Devans, Nabby, m. Capt. Jonathan Chapman.
Deverell, J. Mr. J. D., watchmaker, to Miss Hannah Hewes. (S. Aug. 15, 1789.)

Dew, Hendric. At New Haven, Mr. H. D. to Miss Hannah Gilbert. (S. Apr. 21, 1792.)

Dexter, Catharine Maria, m. Artemas Ward, jun.

Dexter, Edward. At Providence, Mr. E. D., merchant, to Miss Abigail Smith. (S. Dec. 28, 1793.)

Dexter, John. At Cumberland, Mr. J. D. to Miss Lucy Dexter. (W. Feb. 12, 1794.)

Dexter, Lewis. At North Providence, Mr. L. D. to Miss Lydia Comstock. (W. Feb. 13, 1793.)

Dexter, Lucy, m. John Dexter.

Dexter, Nancy, m. Abraham Bishop.

Dexter, Samuel. S. D., Esq., of Albany, in the State of New York, to Miss Eliza Province, of this town. (W. June 16, 1790.)

Dickerson, Rev. Timothy. At Holliston, the Rev. T. D. to Miss Margaret Prentiss, daughter of the late Rev. Joshua Prentiss. (S. Dec. 12, 1789.)

Dickinson, Patty, m. John Barrett.

Dickman, Joseph. Last Thursday se'ennight, Mr. J. D. to Miss Mary Tucker. (S. Mar. 18, 1786.)

Dickman, Thomas. In this town, Mr. T. D. to Miss Betsy Getchell. (S. Dec. 8, 1792.)

Dickman, Thomas. At Springfield, Mr. T. D., printer, of Greenfield, to Miss Nancy Church, eldest daughter of Major Moses Church, of Springfield. (W. Sept. 10, 1794.)

Dilingham, Esther, m. Philip Crandon.

Dillaway, Thomas. Mr. T. D. to Miss Hannah Domac, both of this town. (W. Jan. 26, 1791.)

Dilliway, Hannah, m. John Somes, jun.

Dills, Mrs., m. Rev. President Witherspoon.

Dissotway, Violetta, m. James Briton.

Dixcey, Hannah, m. Mr. P. J. G. de Nancrede.

Doak, William D. At Haverhill, Mr. W. D. D., merchant, to Miss Polly Webster. (S. Mar. 1, 1794.)

Doan, John. In this town, by the Rev. Dr. Stillman, Mr. J. D., of Roxbury, to Miss Percis Crafts, of this town. (S. May 10, 1794.)

Dodd, John. At Danbury, Mr. J. D. to Miss Anne M. Lean. (W. Oct. 17, 1792.)

Dodge, Mary, m. Mr. Balding.

Dogget, Noah. Mr. N. D. to Miss Ruthe Lines. (S. June 8, 1793.)

Dogget, William. By the Rev. Mr. Clarke, Mr. W. D. to Mrs. Mary Russell, both of this town. (W. March 17, 1790.)

Doggett, Henry. In Charleston (S. Carolina), Mr. H. D., merchant, formerly of this town, to Miss Nancy Relfe, of that place. (W. Oct. 21, 1789.)

Doll, Adam. At Kingston, Ulster-Country, Mr. A. D. to Miss Cornecia Tappan. (S. June 23, 1792.)

Dolliver, Capt. William, jun. At Gloucester, Capt. W. D., jun., to Miss Sally Foster, daughter of Col. Joseph Foster, of that place. (S. Aug. 28, 1790.)

Domac, Hannah, m. Thomas Dillaway.

Donielson, Mrs. Eliza, m. Capt. William Eaton.

Donnells, Mrs. Mary, m. James Perkins.

Dorr, Nancy, m. Caleb Clapp.

Dorr, William. By the Rev. Mr. West, Mr. W. D. to Miss Lucinda Davis, daughter of Amassa Davis, Esq., of this town. (S. Nov. 20, 1790.)

Dorsey, Vachel. At Baltimore, Mr. V. D. to Miss Nancy Poole. (S. Apr. 7, 1792.)

D'Orville, Matthew Dennison. In this town, by the Rev. Dr. Lathrop, Mr. M. D. D'O., of Charleston, S. C., to Miss Martha Webb, of Boston. (S. Nov. 8, 1794.)

Doty, Theodore. At New Bedford, Mr. T. D. to Miss Phebe Taber (W. Dec. 25, 1793.)

Douglass, John. In New York, Mr. J. D., of Boston, to Miss Sarah Cannon, of Corlaer's-Hook. (W. Jan. 18, 1792.)

Dow, Ruth, m. Thomas Marshall.

Downs, Elizabeth, m. Francis Wheston.

Downs, Mary, m. Christopher Beal.

Dowse, Edward. In this town, E. D., Esq., to Miss Sally Phillips, daughter of the Hon. William Phillips, Esq. (S. Feb. 27, 1790.)

Dowse, Eliza, m. Joseph Sprague.

Draper, William. [In this town] Mr. W. D. to Miss Hannah Harris. (W. Oct. 26, 1791.)

Drebert, Christain. At Baltimore, Mr. C. D. to Miss Mary Forney. (W. July 4, 1792.)

Drew, Capt. At New York, Capt. D., of the British Navy, to Miss Watkins. (W. May 2, 1792.)

Drew, Betsy, m. Capt. Samuel Jeffers.

Drew, Capt. Clark. At Duxborough, Capt. C. D. to Miss Betsey Bosworth, daughter to Capt. N. Bosworth, late of this town. (W. Jan. 9, 1793.)

Drew, Capt. Rubran. At Duxbury, Capt. R. D. to Miss Sally Loring, daughter to Deacon Loring. (W. Feb. 27 1792.)

Driver, Jenny, m. Jesse Spir.

Drury, Abijah. Mr. A. D. to Miss Kezia Wheelock. (W. March 14, 1792.) At Shrewsbury implied.

Duane, James, jun. At New York, J. D. jun., Esq., to Mrs. Mariann Bowers. (W. Dec. 19, 1792.)

Duane, Polly, m. Major William North.

Dubalett, John. Mr. J. D. to Miss Sally Boit. (W. June 16, 1790.)

Duchemin, Francois. At Baltimore, Mr. F. D., an eminent merchant of Port-au-Prince, to Miss Catherine Maenge. (W. Jan. 30, 1793.)

Dunbar, Mr. At Plymouth, Mr. D., Attorney at Law, to Miss Nancy Crombie. (S. July 12, 1794.)

Dunbar, James. Last evening, Mr. J. D. to Miss Sally Templeton, both of this town. (W. March 28, 1792.)

Duncan, Elizabeth, m. John Thaxter.

Duncan, Robert. At Newgrantham (N. H.), R. D., Esq., to the amiable widow of his late brother, Samuel Duncan, Esq. (S. Oct. 25, 1794.)

Duncan, William. At Philadelphia, Mr. W. D. to Miss Polly Moulder. (S. Nov. 17, 1792.)

Dunham, Jesse. [At Newport] Mr. J. D. to Miss Betsey Fell. (W. Oct. 1, 1794.)

Dunkin, Robert H. At New York, R. H. D., Esq., of Philadelphia, to Miss Watkins, of New York. (W. Jan. 23, 1793.)

Dunnels, Samuel. In this town, Mr. S. D. to Miss Deborah Kneeland. (S. July 5, 1794.)

Dunton, Ruth, m. Thomas P. Clark.

Durant, Cornelius. The 20th inst., C. D., Esq., of the island of St. Croix, to Miss Mary Fenno, of this town. (W. May 24, 1786.)

Durivage, Nicholas. At Dedham, Mons., N. D. to Miss Nancy Baker. (W. Jan. 30, 1788.)

The town records of Dedham read: By the Revd Mr Haven, Jany 23, 1788, Francois Nicolas Caillian Durivage and Miss Anna Baker, both of Dedham.

Durton, Lt. Ebenezer. At Concord (N H.), Lt. E. D., to Miss Betsy Bryant. (S. Nov. 22, 1794.)

Duteau, Catharine, m. Isaac Stevens.

Duton, Susanna, m. Russel Meers.

Dyer, Elizabeth, m. Luther Brownell.

Dyer, John. In this town, on Sunday evening last, Mr. J. D., to Miss Polly Jasper, both of this town. (S. March 31, 1792.)

Dyer, Mary, m. Capt. Stephen Smith.

Dwight, Elizabeth, m. William W. Woolsey.

Dwight, Henry. At West-Springfield, Mr. H. D., to Miss Lydia Day. (S. Oct. 1, 1791.)

Dwight, James. At Portland, Mr. J. D., of Springfield, to Miss Sanford, of Portland. (W. Oct. 8, 1794.)

Dwight, Jonathan. At Hartford, Mr. J. D., of Springfield, merchant, to Miss Margaret Van Vauxter Vanderspeigel, (W. April 21, 1790.)

Dwight, Josiah. At Sandwich, Mr. J. D., of Stockbridge, to Miss Caroline Williams. (S. May 23, 1789.)

Dwight, Polly, m. Benjamin Powel.

Dwight, Theodore. At Hartford (C.), T. D., Esq., to Miss Abby Aslop. (W. Sept. 26, 1792.)

Earl, Rebecca, m. Dame Corey.

Easton, Dr. Peter. At Nantucket, Dr. P. E., to Miss Mary Coffin, eldest daughter of Peleg Coffin, Esq.

Eaton, Mr. At Stoughton, Mr. E., of Easton, merchant, to Mrs. Hixon, widow of the late Richard Hixon, deceased; a lady possessed of every accomplishment, external and mental, requisite to soften the hymenial chains. (W. Feb. 23, 1785.)

Eaton, Ebenezer, In this town, Mr. E. E., to Miss Polly Allen. (S. March 29, 1794.)

Eaton, Thankful, m. Samuel Lawson.

Eaton, Captain William. At Windsor [Vt.], Capt. W. E., to Mrs. Eliza Donielson, relict of the late Hon. Timothy Donielson. (W. Sept. 5, 1792.)

Eaton, William. At Newport, Mr. W. E., to Miss Eliza Oldfield. (W. Oct. 31, 1792.)

Eayres, Thomas. By the Rev. Mr. James Freeman, Mr. T. E., to Miss Fannie Revere, both of this town. (W. May 28, 1788.)

Eddy, Sally, m. John Greenman.

Edes, Hannah, m. Thomas Lillie.

Edes, Isaac. Mr. I. E., to Miss Sally Pierce. (W. Sept. 21, 1791.

Edes, Captain Josiah. Capt. J. C., to Miss Polly Allen, both of this town. (S. Jan. 23, 1790.)

Edes, Mrs. Mary, m. John Stanton.

Edes, Polly Harris, m. Capt. Isaac Pepper.

Edey, Samuel. At Providence, S. E., Esq., to Miss Betsey Bucklin. (W. Nov. 21, 1792.)

Edmonds, Joseph. Mr. J. E., to Miss Hannah Warner. (S. June 28, 1794.)

Edmunds, Joseph. At Roxbury, Mr. J. E., to Miss Nancy Shepherd. (S. April 27, 1793.)

Edson, Josiah. At Bridgewater, Mr. J. E., to Miss Susanna Richards. (S. Feb. 26, 1791.)

Edson, Mrs. Sally, m. Joseph Cross.

Edwards, Richard. R. E., Esq , to Miss Griffin, of Connecticut. (W. Feb. 16, 1791.)

Edwards, Susannah, m. Simeon Wyman.

Edwards, William. At Northampton, Mr. W. E., to Miss Rebecca Tappan. (W. Nov. 20, 1793.)

Eldridge, William. At Groton (Con.), Mr. W. E., to Miss Eliza Avery. (S. Oct. 4, 1794.)

Eliot, Ruthy, m. Capt. Thomas Knox.

Eliot, Samuel. At Newbury, Mr. S. E., of this town, merchant, to Miss Katherine Atkins. (W. May 24, 1786.)

Eliot, Sukey, m. Dr. David Hull.

Elkins, Nabby, m. George C. Ward.

Elkins, Mrs. Sarah, m. Chase Taylor.

Ellery, Almy, m. William Stedman.

Ellery, Christopher. At Newport, C. E., Esq., to Miss Clarissa Bird, youngest daughter of Mr. Nathaniel Bird, merchant. (S. Nov. 10, 1792.)

Ellery, Edmund Trowbridge. At Newport, E. T. Ellery, Esq., to Miss Katy Almy. (W. Oct. 17, 1792.)

Elliot, Mrs. Elizabeth, m. Edward Pope.

Elliot, Dr. Ephraim. Dr. E. E., to Miss Elizabeth Fleet, daughter to Mr. John Fleet, Printer. (S. Dec. 19, 1789.)

Elliot, Rev. John. At East-Guilford, Rev. J. E., to Miss Sally Norton. (W. Dec. 4, 1793.)

Elliot, Sally, m. Thomas H. Perkins.

Ellis, Elisha. Mr. E. E., to Miss Polly Underwood [both of this town]. (S. Aug. 6, 1791.)

Ellis, William. In this town, Mr. W. E., to Mrs. Lydia Collins, both of this town. (S. Nov. 16, 1793.)

Ellison, William, jun. In this town, Mr. W. E., jun., to Miss Polly Jackson. (W. June 18, 1794.)

Elmendorph, Peter Ed. At Albany, P. E. E., Esq., of Troy, to Miss Betsy Van Rensselear, daughter of Philip Van Rensselear, Esq., of the former place. (W. March 20, 1793.)

Elmslie, Hannah, m. Charles Godfried Paleske.

Elrins, Polly, m. Andrew Slewman.

Ely, Edwards. At Danbury, Mr. E. E., Printer, to Miss Peck. (S. Jan. 21, 1792.)

Emerson, Polly, m. Seth Russell.

Emerson, Doctor Samuel. At York, the 14th inst., by the Rev. Mr. Lankton, Doctor S. E., of Wells, to the amiable Miss Olive Barrell, daughter of Nathaniel Barrell, Esq., of that town. (S. Sept. 3, 1791.)

Emery, Samuel. Last Thursday evening, Mr. S. E., merchant, to Miss Polly Appleton, eldest daughter of Nathaniel Appleton, Esq. (S. May 7, 1785.)

Emlay, Theodosia, m. Thomas Fitzheimer.

Emmons, Joshua. [In this town] Mr. J. E , to Miss Bulfinch. (S. Aug. 16, 1794.)

Emmons, Nathaniel. On Thursday evening, by the Rev. Dr. Stillman, Mr. N. E. to Miss Sukey Hitchins (both of this town). (S. Nov. 12, 1791.)

Ervin, Nabby, m. George Reynolds.

Erving, John, jun. Mr. J. E., jun., merchant, to Miss Nancy Sheaffe, of this town. (S. Sept. 30, 1786.)

Eustis, Jacob. In this town, Mr. J. E. to Miss Eliza Saunders Gray. (S. Aug. 9, 1794.)

Eustis, Nancy m. Henry S. Langdon.

Eustis, Prudence, m. Francis Amory.

Eustis, William. Mr. W. E. to Miss Deborah Bennet [both of this town]. . (W. Nov. 17, 1790.)

Eustis, William. At Newton, Mr. W. E. to Miss Anna Morse. (S. Nov. 15, 1794.)

Evans, Israel. At Charlestown, Mr. I. E. to Miss Huldah Kent, of that place. (S. May 6, 1786.)

Eyres, Polly, m. Isaac Bowers.

Fairbanks, Ithamar. At Milton, Mr. I. F. to Miss Jerusha Williams. (S. Dec. 27, 1788.)

Fairchild, N. At Huntington, Mr. N. F. to Miss Sarah Bennett. (S. April 14, 1792.)

Fairfield, Rev. John. At Roxbury, on Thursday last, the Rev. J. F., of Pepperrelborough, to Miss Martha Ruggles, of Roxbury. (S. Sept. 17, 1785.)

Fairfield, Sally, m. Capt. Jonathan Gardner.

Falconet, John-Lewis-Theodore Depalizeux. At London, J. L. T. D. F., to the amiable Miss Anne Hunter, of Newport, Rhode Island. (W. Nov. 24, 1790.)

Fales, Nancy, m. Edward Sisson.

Farley, Capt. Daniel. At Newburyport, Capt. D. F., of Ipswich, to Mrs. Rebecca Noyes. (W. Dec. 5, 1792.)

Farley, Sally, m. James Phillips.

Farley, Susannah, m. William Burley.

Farn, Susannah, m. Joseph Jones.

Farnam, Nancy, m. Edward Cole.

Farrar, Mary, m. Gen. James Read.

Farrington, Daniel. At Taunton, Mr. D. F. to Miss Rebecca Wilde. (W. May 16, 1792.)

Farrington, Sally, m. Mamy Masson.

Farrond, Stephen. At Newport, Mr. S. F., of New Jersey, to Miss Mary Clark. (W. Oct. 27, 1790.)

Faulkner, Mary Arrowsmith, m. John Henry Flieger.

Faxon, Benjamin. In this town, Mr. B. F. to Miss Rebecca Stone. (W. Jan. 11, 1792.)

Faxon, Caleb. At Dedham, Mr. C. F. to Miss Lydia Hathaway. (W. Dec. 11, 1793.)

Faxton, Unice, m. James Gridley.

Fay, Dr. Nahum. At Charlestown, Dr. N. F. to Miss Sally Putnam. (S. June 21, 1794.)
Fay, Patty, m. Liscomb Bingham.
Fell, Betsey, m. Jesse Dunbar.
Fellowes, Abigail, m. Perrin May.
Fellowes, Betsy, m. David Bradlee, jun.
Fellows, Betsey, m. Joshua Prior.
Fellows, Lydia, m. Jonathan Amory.
Fellows, Sally, m. Nathaniel Ruggles.
Felt, Benjamin. At Salem, Mr. B. F. to Miss Sally Ward. (W. Oct. 29, 1794.)
Fenden, B., m. William Martin.
Fenner, Samuel. At Weymouth, Mr. S. F. to Miss Sukey Humphrey, both of that place. (W. July 9, 1794.)
Fenno, Jesse. At Quincey, Mr. J. F. to Miss Eliza Arnold, of that place. (W. Oct. 16, 1793.)
Fenno, John. At Noodle's Island, J. F., of Stoughton, to Miss Olive Pratt. (S. Dec. 14, 1793.)
Fenno, Mary, m. Cornelius Durant.
Fernald, Polly, m. Capt. Tristram Jorden.
Fernald, William Wentworth. At Kittery, Mr. W. W. F. to the amiable Miss Wait Salisbury. (S. Dec. 5, 1789.)
Ferry, John. [In this town] Mr. J. F. to Miss Anna Dart. (S. Apr. 5, 1794.)
Fettiplace, Edward. At Marblehead, E. F., Esq., to Mrs. Sarah Bowden. (W. Sept. 17, 1794.)
Few, Hon. Mr. At New York, Hon. Mr. F., Delegate in Congress, from Georgia, to Miss Nicholson, daughter of Commodore Nicholson. (S. June 21, 1788.)
William Few, U. S. Senator. See also Sēney, Hon. Joshua.
Field, Mary, m. Samuel Kenney.
Field, Stephen. [At Salem] Mr. S. F. to Miss Sally Hovey. (W. Oct. 29, 1794.)
Finney, Jeremiah. At Bristol (R. I.), Mr. J. F., to Mrs. Cay. (S. April 14, 1792.)
Fisher, James. At Stoughton, Mr. J. F., gentleman, deputy sheriff, collector and constable, to Miss Polly Tucker, both of that place. (W. March 16, 1791.)

Fisk, Barbary, m. Capt. Christopher Knight.

Fisk, Ede, m. Aron Whitney.

Fisk, John. At Marblehead, J. F., Esq., to Mrs. Gerry, widow of the late John Gerry, Esq. (W. June 28, 1786.)

Fisk, Dr. Joseph, jun. At Lexington, Dr. J. F., jun., to Miss Betsy Stone. (S. Aug. 16, 1794.)

Fisk, Sally, m. Ebenezer Putnam.

Fisk, Sybil, m. Timothy Kinsley.

Fiske, Abigail, m. Isaac Lampson.

Fiske, Lucretia, m. Samuel Janes.

Fitch, Beriah. [At Nantucket] Mr. B. F. to Miss Sally Delano. (W. Sept. 14, 1793.)

Fitch, Eunice, m. Andrew Hall.

Fitch, Hannah Brown, m. Ezekiel Hersy Derby.

Fitzgerald, Mrs. Honour, m. Rev. John Browne.

Fitzheimer, Thomas. At Trenton, Mr. T. F., merchant, of Philadelphia, to Miss Theodosia Emlay, of that place. (S. Nov. 17, 1792.)

Flagg, Grace S., m. Aaron Mann.

Flagg, Josiah, Jr. By the Rev. Mr. Parker, J. F. Jr., S. D., to Miss Hannah Collins, daughter of the late Capt. Palfry Collins. (W. Oct. 13, 1790.)

Flagg, Peggy, m. John Fontemoi.

Flagg, Samuel. At Charleston (S. C.), Mr. S. F., dentist, late of this town, to Miss Lucy Megraw, of that city. (W. Feb. 13, 1793.)

Flagg, Susanna, m. James Gardner.

Flahaven, Miss, m. Matthew Carey.

Flanlin, Eunice, m. Benjamin Callender.

Fleet, Elizabeth, m. Dr. Ephraim Elliot.

Fletcher, Capt. Patrick. Capt. P. F. to Miss Sally Bradlee, eldest daughter of Capt. David Bradlee, of this town, wine-merchant. (S. Oct. 15, 1785.)

Fletcher, Sally, m. Joseph Wheaton.

Fletcher, Mrs. Sarah, m. Oliver Leonard.

Flieger, John Henry. [At Halifax] Mr. J. H. F. to Miss Mary Arrowsmith Faulkner. (W. Nov. 7, 1792.)

Flint, Lydia, m. Oliver Munroe.

Flynn, Daniel Finaly. On Monday evening last, Mr. D. F. F. to Miss Peggy Conner. (W. May 11, 1791.)

Fobes, Mary, m. Rev. Elijah Leanord.

Foble, John. In this town, Mr. J. F. to Miss Abigail Simpson. (S. June 16, 1792.)

Folgier, Capt. David. At Nantucket, Capt. D. F. to Miss Eliza Moores. (S. Dec. 7, 1793.)

Folsom, Col. Nathaniel. At Portsmouth, Col. N. F. to Miss Olive Rindge. (S. Aug. 29, 1789.)

Fontemoi, John. Mr. J. F. to Miss Peggy Flagg. (S. Jan. 20, 1787.)

S. May 31, 1788, the following occurs: Died. In this town, M. John Emanuel Fontemoing, aged thirty-two.

Fontemoing, Mrs. Margaret, m. Francis Garaux.

Foord, Thomas. At Scituate, Mr. T. F. of Duxbury, to Miss Abigail Church. (S. July 19, 1794.)

Foot, Abel. At Danbury, Mr. A. F. to Miss Jennet Platt. (S. April 7, 1792.)

Forbes, Rev. Eli. The Rev. E. F., of Gloucester, to Mrs. Baldwin, of Brookfield. (S. Dec. 28, 1793.)

Forbes, Rev. Eli. At Brookfield, Rev. E. F., of Gloucester, to Mrs. Lucy Baldwin. (W. Jan. 8, 1794.)

Forbes, Hannah, m. Nahum Gale.

Force, Catherine, m. Daniel Hall.

Ford, Bethany, m. Seth Ford.

Ford, John. [At Marsfield] Mr. J. F. to Miss Marcey L. Baker. (W. March 20, 1793.)

Ford, Nancy, m. Joshua Tappan.

Ford, Peggy, m. Zachariah Atwood.

Ford, Polly, m. Nathaniel Freeman, jun.

Ford, Priscilla, m. Capt. Wench.

Ford, Seth. At Marshfield, Mr. J. F., to Miss Bethany Ford. (W. March 20, 1793.)

Forman, Elenora, m. Captian Philip Freneau.

Forney, Mary, m. Christian Drebert.

Forrest, Hon. Uriah. In Maryland, Hon. U. F., to Miss Plater. (S. Nov. 7, 1789.)

Forsdick, Sally, m. David Pease.

Forward, Capt. Amos. At Westfield, Capt. A. F., aged 84,

to Mrs. Moore, aged 74. Who would imagine this happy couple were *Forward?* But so it is, they are. (W. Nov. 9, 1791.)

Fosdick, Joseph. In this town, Mr. J. F. to Miss Charlotte Davis, daughter to Mr. Edward Davis, merchant. (W. Oct. 30, 1793.)

Fosdick, Lydia, m. Lewis Lambert Macallier.

Fosdick, Sally, m. James Frothingham, jun.

Foster, Hannah, m, Benjamin Daland.

Foster, Jacob. At Pembroke, Mr. J. F., of Scituate, to Joanna Stevens, of that place. (S. April 6, 1793.)

Foster, Rev. John. Last Thursday evening, the Reverend J. F., of Cambridge, to the amiable Miss Hannah Webster, of Boston, a young lady of superior sense and merit. (S. April 9, 1785.)

Foster, John. At Duxborough, Mr. J. F., of Scituate, to Miss Abigail Sutherd, of that place. (S. April 6, 1793.)

Foster, John. [At Salem] Mr. J. F. to Miss Polly Holt. (S. Aug. 9, 1794.)

Foster, Capt. John. At Salem, Capt. J. F. to Miss Polly Burchmore. (S. Aug. 9, 1794.)

Foster, Nathan. In this town, Mr. N. F. to Miss Hannah Trow, both of this town. (W. Dec. 31, 1794.)

Foster, Polly, m. Ebenezer Brewer.

Foster, Sally, m. Harrison Gray Otis.

Foster, Sally, m. Joseph Brown.

Foster, Sally, m. Capt. William Dolliver.

Foster, Sukey, m. Rev. Frederick Parker.

Fowle, Henry. [In this town] Mr. H. F. to Miss Betsy Bently. (S. Nov. 7, 1789.)

Fowle, Jeremiah. At Watertown, Mr. J. F., to Miss Polly Capen, daughter of Major Capen. (S. Jan. 5, 1788.)

Fowle, Jonathan. In this town, Mr. J. F. to Miss Sally Makepeace. (W. June 28, 1786.)

Fowle, Margaret, m. Loammi Baldwin.

Fox, John. In this town, Mr. J. F. to Miss Marcy Laha. (W. Nov. 19, 1788.)

Fox, John. Mr. J. F., merchant, to Miss Abigail Bayley, both of this town. (W. March 5, 1794.)

Fox, Maria, m. Capt. Joseph Cowdin.

Fox, Nancy, m. Nathan Western.

Fox, Richard. In this town, Mr. R. F. to Miss Rachel Pierson. (W. March 5, 1788.)

Fox, Sarah, m. Ruggles Green.

Francis, Caleb. Mr. C. F. to Miss Polly Rose of this town. (W. May 13, 1789.)

Francis, John. At Providence, J. F., Esq., merchant, to Miss Abby Brown, daughter of John Brown, Esq. (W. Jan. 16, 1788.)

Francis, John. Mr. J. F. to Miss Rebecca Corbet [both] of this town. (W. April 9, 1794.)

Francis, Joseph. In this town, Mr. J. F. to Miss Mary Gendell. (S. July 13, 1793.)

Francis, Silas. Mr. S. F. to Miss Nancy Steele. (W. Sept. 10, 1794.)

At Newbury-Port implied. Repeated. S. Sept. 20.

Francis, Sophia, m. George Harrison.

Franklin, Rebecca, m. John Townsend.

Frayatt, Betsey, m. Capt. John Strode.

Freeman, Betsey, m. Caleb Aspinwall.

Freeman, Constant. In this town, by the Rev. Mr. Elliot, C. F., Esq., to Mrs. Susannah Palfrey. (W. Feb. 1, 1792.)

Freeman, Experience, m. Watson Freeman.

Freeman, Rev. James. The Rev. J. F. to Mrs. Martha Clarke. (S. July 19, 1788.)

Of King's chapel, married 17 July.

Freeman, Jonathan, jun. Mr. J. F., jun., merchant, to Mrs. Abigail Brown, widow of the late Enoch Brown, Esq. (W. March 26, 1788.)

Abigail Kendrick of Newton.—Bridgman's King's chapel inscr., p. 233.

Freeman, Nabby, m. Major Abraham Williams.

Freeman, Nathaniel. In this town, by the Rev. Doctor Howard, Mr. N. F., merchant, to Miss Sukey Nye, both of this town. (W. Jan. 25, 1792.)

Freeman, Nathaniel, jun. N. F., jun., Esq., of Sandwich, to Miss Polly Ford, of this town. (W. June 29, 1791.)

Freeman, Watson. Mr. W. F. to Miss Sally Hinkley, of Barnstable. (W. May 8, 1793.)

Freeman, Watson. At Sandwich, Mr. W. F., of this town, to Miss Experience Freeman, daughter of Seth Freeman, Esq., of the first place. (S. Nov. 22, 1794.)

French, Theodore. [In this town] Mr. T. F. to Miss Elizabeth Dawes. (S. July 5, 1794.)

French, Zadock. In this town, Mr. Z. F., distiller, to the amiable Miss Bulah Smith. (W. Oct. 2, 1793.)

Freneau, Captain Philip. In Monmouth county (N. J.), Captain P. F. to Miss Elenora Forman. (W. May 5, 1790.)

Frobisher, William. Mr. W. F. to Miss Nancy Corbet. (S. Jan. 20, 1787.)

Frost, Mrs. Dorcas, m. Asa Lapham.

Frost, Dea. Ephraim. [In this town] Dea. E. F. to Miss Boylston. (W. June 11, 1794.)

Frost, George. At Portsmouth, Mr. G. F., mer., Berwick, to Miss Sally Boles. (S. Sept. 20, 1794.)

Frost, Hannah, m. Jacob Kuhn.

Frothingham, Dabby, m. Amos Tufts.

Frothingham, James, jun. At Charlestown, Mr. J. F., jun., to Miss Sally Fosdick, both of that town. (W. May 24, 1786.)

Frothingham, John. Last evening, J. F., of Falmouth, Esq., to the amiable Miss Patty May, daughter of Samuel May, Esq., of this town. (W. Sept. 14, 1785.)

Frothingham, Nathaniel. Mr. N. F. to Miss Polly Townshend, of this town. (W. Jan. 4, 1786.)

Frothingham, Suckey, m. John Kettle.

Fuller, Katy, m. Rev. Ebenezer Wight.

Fullerton, Eliza, m. Capt Gardner Hammond.

Furman, Miss, m. William Boyd.

Furniss, Rebecca, m. Moses Beaujean.

Frye, Betsy, m. Dr. Nathan Lukeman.

Frye, Lucy, m. Solomon Abbot.

Gade, Peter. [In this town] Mr. P. G., to Miss Sukey Ridgaway. (W. Jan. 9, 1793.)

Gale, Nahum. [At Westborough] Mr. N. G., to Miss Hannah Forbes. (W. Dec. 19, 1792.)

Gale, Susannah, m. Rev. Mr. Morrill.

Gallaten, Hon. Albert. At New York, Hon. A. G., Esq., senator of the United States for Pennsylvania, to Miss Nicholson, daughter to James Nicholson, Esq. (S. Nov. 23, 1793.)

Galley, Hannah, m. James Carter Singleton.

Gallison, Charlotte, m. Sylvanus Gray.

Gallup, Col. Oliver. At Windsor (Vermont), Col. O. G., of Hartland, to Miss Bethiah Homer, of Boston. (W. Jan. 4, 1792.)

Garaux, Francis. In this town, Mr. F. G. to Mrs. Margaret Fontimoing. (S. March 12, 1791.)

Gardiner, Betsey, m. Stephen Crane.

Gardiner, Lucy, m. Thomas Boone.

Gardiner, Dr. Walter C. At Newport, Dr. W. C. G. to Miss Eliza Wickham. (W. May 23, 1792.)

Gardner, Mrs. Alice, m. James Gardner.

Gardner, Ann, m. Thomas Howe.

Gardner, Bethuel. Mr. B. G. to Miss Sally Morris. (S. Dec. 7, 1793.)
At Nantucket?

Gardner, Eliakim. Mr. E. G. to Miss Pamelia Gardner. (S. Dec. 7, 1793.)
At Nantucket?

Gardner, James. Mr. J. G. to Mrs. Alice Gardner, of this town. (S. Nov. 1, 1788.)

Gore, Katy, m. Jonathan Hunnewell.

Gore, Katy, m. Samuel Torrey.

Gorham, Miss, m. Warham Parker.

Gorham, Ann, m. Peter C. Brown.

Gorham, Benjamin. Mr. B. G. to Mrs. Deborah Crocker. (W. Sept. 16, 1789.) At Barnstable implied.

Gorham, Capt. Job. In this town last Saturday evening, by the Rev. Dr. Lathrop, Capt. J. G. to the amiable Miss Rebecca Davis, both of Barnstable. (W. Sept. 6, 1786.)

Gorham, Mary, m. George Bartlett.

Gorham, Nathaniel. At Charlestown, last evening, by the Rev. Dr. Morse, N. G., Esq., to Miss Ruth Wood, eldest daughter of Col. David Wood, of Charlestown. (W. Feb. 12, 1794.)

Gould, Nathaniel. At Danvers, Mr. N. G. to Miss Betsey Porter. (S. Feb. 16, 1793.)

Gould, Reuben. At Chelmsford, Mr. R. G. to Miss Patty Phillips. (S. May 29, 1790.)

Gould, Sarah, m. Ebenezer Pool.

Goulding, Mrs., m. Col. Job Cushing.

Goulding, Mrs. Azubah, m. Capt. Joseph Torrey.

Gotte, Hannah, m. William Boylston.

Grace, William. In England, Mr. W. G. to Miss M. Tangshaw. His father is his brother, and her mother is his sister! However strange the above circumstance may appear, it is all brought about by the wonderful effects of matrimony. (W. March 28, 1792.)

Graham, Asa. Mr. A. G. to Miss Sally West. (S. June 28, 1794.)
At Concord (N. H.), implied.

Graham, John. Mr. J. G. to Miss Nabby Brown, of this town. (W. Oct. 6, 1790.)

Grant, Abigail, m. John Coffin Jones.

Grant, Betsy, m. Samuel Snelling.

Grant, William. At New-York, Mr. W. G., of St. Augustine, to Miss Ann Sample, of that city. (S. Nov. 5, 1791.)

Graves, Electra, m. James Orton.

Graves, John Bonon. Last Sunday evening, J. B. G., Esq., Consul of South-Carolina, from the United States of Holland, to Miss Sally Atwood, of this town. (W. July 23, 1788.)

Gray, Edward. E. G. Esq., Attorney at Law, to Miss Sukey Turrell, daughter of the late Joseph Turrell, Esq. (S. April 17, 1790.)

Gray, Eliza Saunders, m. Jacob Eustis.

Gray, Francis. On Sunday Evening, Mr. F. G., merchant, to Miss Polly Young. (W. Sept. 7, 1785.)

Gray, Hannah, m. Hon. James Willson.

Gray, Capt. John. In this town, on Sunday evening, Capt. J. G., merchant, to Miss Polly Roberts, both of this town. W. Feb. 9, 1791.)

Gray, Patty, m. Dr. Samuel Danforth.

Gray, Polly, m. Barnabas Bidwell.

Gray, Rev. Robert. In Charlestown, the Rev. R. G., of Dover, New Hampshire, to Miss Lydia Tufts, daughter of Mr. John Tufts, of that town. (S. March 31, 1787.)

Gray, Capt. Robert. [In this town] Capt. R. G. to Miss Martha Atkins. (S. Feb. 15, 1794.)

Gray, Samuel. At Salem, Mr. S. G., merchant, to Miss Nancy Orne, of that town. (S. Nov. 10, 1787.)

Gray, Sylvanus. At Marblehead, Mr. S. G., of this town, to Miss Charlotte Gallison. (W. Sept. 3, 1794).

Gray, Thomas. At Barnstable, Mr. T. G., of Yarmouth, to Miss Ruth Davis. (S. July 18, 1789.)

Gray, Rev. Thomas. On Thursday evening last, the Rev. T. G. to Miss Debby Stillman, youngest daughter of the Rev. Dr. Stillman. (S. May 25, 1793.)

Gray, Winthrop. At Salem, W. G. Esq., to Miss Eliza Putnam. (S. Oct. 29, 1791.)

Greaton, Katy, m. James Dana.

Greaton, Mrs. Sarah, m. Samuel Ridgway.

Greeanleaf, John. At Newbury-Port, Mr. J. G., merchant, to Mrs. Elizabeth Greenleaf. (W. Jan. 15, 1794.)

Greele, Moses. At Sandy River, Mr. M. G., aged 88, to an agreeable widow of about 56. (S. May 11, 1793.)

Greely, Hannah, m. William Stevenson.

Greely, Mrs. Mary, m. Col. Jonathan Glover.

Greely, Nancy, m. Caleb Loring.

Green, Dr. Isaac. In this town, Dr. I. G., of Windsor, to Miss Nancy Barrett, daughter of Samuel Barrett, Esq., of this town. (S. Jan. 21, 1792.)

Green, Jeremiah. At East Greenwich, Mr. J. G. to Miss Lydia Arnold. (W. Oct. 27, 1790.)
In Rhode Island.

Green, Joel. In Baltimore county, Mr. J. G. to Miss Elizabeth Buck. (W. April 25, 1792.)

Green, Maria, m. Benjamin Sumner.

Green, Martha, m. Capt. Lewis Carnes.

Green, Nathaniel. [At Shrewsbury] Mr. N. G. to Miss Lucy Stone. (S. June 16, 1792.)

Green, Polly, m. William Hill.

Green, Ruggles. [At Bernardston] Mr. R. G. to Miss Sarah Fox. (W. Dec. 11, 1793.)

Greene, Timothy. At Providence, T. G., Esq., of Worcester, to Miss Polly Martin, of Providence. (S. March 16, 1793.)

Greenleaf, Miss, m. John Appleton.

Greenleaf, Mrs. Elizabeth, m. John Greeanleaf.

Greenleaf, Mary, m. Capt. Nathaniel Thwing.

Greenleaf, Polly, m. Charles Sigourney.

Greenleaf, Rebecca, m. Noah Webster, jr.

Greenleaf, Thomas. In this town, Mr. T. G. to Miss Polly Price, daughter of Ezekiel Price, Esq. (W. Apr. 25, 1787.)

Greenleaf, Thomas. At New York, Mr. T. G., Printer, to Miss Nancy Quackenbos. (W. Oct. 26, 1791).

Greenman, John. At Warren, Mr. J. G., of Swansea, to Miss Sally Eddy, of Providence. (S. Nov. 23, 1793.)

Greenough, Mary, m. William Howes.

Greenough, Nancy, m. Elisha Bangs.

Greenough, Rachel, m. Jonas Brooks.

Greenough, Sally, m. William Cordwell.

Greenough, William. [In this town] Mr. W. G., Printer, to Miss Mary More, of this town. (S. April 26, 1794.)

Greenwood, Isaac. At Newport, Mr. I. G., Esq., to Miss Nabby Langley. (W. May 14, 1788.)

Greenwood, John. At New York, Mr. J. G. (dentist), to Miss Betsey Weaver. (W. April 9, 1788.)

Grice, Hannah, m. Samuel Bangs, jun.

Gridley, James. Mr. J. G. to Miss Unice Faxton. (S. March 31, 1792.)

On Sunday last implied.

Gridley, Patty, m. Joseph Howe.

Gridley, Rebecca, m. Ephraim Mills.

Gridley, Richard, jun. By the Rev. Mr. Murray, Mr. R. G., jun., to Miss Sally James. (S. Nov. 2, 1793.)

Griffin, Miss, m. Richard Edwards.

Grough, Catherine, m. John Perry.

Groves, Charles. [In this town] Mr. C. G. to Miss Eliza Wheeler. (W. Jan. 1, 1794.)

Guerney, Mary, m. Thomas Bacon.

Guest, Sally, m. John Campbell.

Gullishan, Ebenezer. [At Newburyport] Mr. E. G. to Miss Eliza Titcomb. (S. Nov. 1, 1794.)

Gulliver, Stephen. In this town. Mr. S. G. to Miss Abigail Levett. (S. Aug. 24, 1793.)

Gummer, James. In this town, Mr. J. G., of Bridgport, Eng., to Miss Sally Viebart, of this town. (S. April 19, 1794.)
See also Viburt.

Hadley, Matty, m. Thomas Stutson.

Hagger, Sally, m. Capt. Moses Tuck.

Haiden, Nancy, m. Jonathan Loring, jun.

Hale, Nancy, m. Jonathan Chadbourne.

Hall, Ammi C. Last Tuesday evening, by the Rev. Mr. Everett, Mr. A. C. H. to the amiable Miss Betsy Seabury, both of this town. (S. April 1, 1786.)

Hall, Andrew. At Medford, on Sunday evening last, Mr. A. H., merchant, to the amiable Miss Eunice Fitch, daughter to Timothy Fitch, Esq. (S. April 25, 1789.)

Hall, Catherine, m. Caleb Gibbs.

Hall, Daniel. At Wrentham, Mr. D. H. to Miss Catherine Force. (S. Feb. 26, 1791.)

Hall, Edward. [At Nantucket], Mr. E. H. to Miss Nabby Townsend. (W. July 17, 1793.)

Hall, Eliza, m. Dr. William Reed.

Hall, John. At Dorchester, by the Rev. Moses Everett, Mr. J. H. to Miss Deborah Allen. (S. May 7, 1791.)

Hall, John. In this town, Mr. J. H. to Miss Betsy Secomb, of Salem. (S. July 9, 1791.)

Hall, Deacon Moses. [In this town] by the Rev. Dr. Stillman, Deacon M. H. to Miss Hannah Bridges, both of this place. (W. Dec. 19, 1792.)

Hall, Parker. P. H., Esq., to Mrs. Crossing. (W. Oct. 27, 1790.)

Hall, Patty, m. William H. Bowers.

Hall, Polly, m. John Breed.

Hall, Rebecca, m. Isaac Parker.

Hall, Sally, m. Samuel Blagge.

Hall, Sally, m. John Kennedy.

Hall, Stephen. At Hingham, Mr. S. H., of this town, to Miss Sally Jacobs of that place. (S. March 31, 1792.)

Hall, Thomas. At Barnstable, by Rev. Mr. Shaw, Mr. T.

H., Printer, of this town to Miss Nabby Thatcher, of that place. (S. Nov. 9, 1793.)

Hall, Zeabilon. At Hingham, Mr. Z. H. to Miss Patty Beals. (S. Nov. 22, 1794.)

Halliburton, Rebecca, m. Capt. Robert Murray.

Halsey, John. [In this town] J. H., Esq., of New-York, to Miss Nancy Crafts, second daughter to Thomas Crafts, Esq. (W. July 16, 1794.)

Halstead, Sarah T., m. John Roach.

Ham, George. [At Portsmouth] Mr. G. H. to Miss Johanna Beck. (S. Nov. 22, 1794.)

Hamblin, Maria, m. Matthew Tasker.

Hamersley, Lucretia, m. Monson Hayt.

Hamilton, Anne, m. James Lyle.

Hammatt, Lydia, m. Capt. Thomas Norton.

Hammond, Abijah. At Newark (N. J.), A. H., Esq., of New-York, to Miss Catharine Ogden, of Newark. (W. Feb. 9, 1791.)

Hammond, Asa. [In this town] Mr. A. H. to Miss Sally Dawes. (W. June 18, 1794.)

Hammond, Benjamin. Mr. B. H. to Miss Sally Nichols, daughter of Mr. S. N. (W. April 4, 1792.)
At Newport implied.

Hammond, Capt. Gardner. In this town, Capt. G. H. to Miss Eliza Fullerton. (W. April 12, 1794.)

Hammond, George. At Philadelphia, G. H., Esquire, his Britannic Majesty's Minister Plenipotentiary to the United States, to Miss Peggy Allen, of that place. W. May 29, (1793.)

Hamock, Mrs. Sally, m. Elijah Brigham.

Hancock, Nathaniel. In this town, Mr. N. H., Miniature Painter, to Miss Betsey Welsh. (W. May 25, 1791.)

Handy, Merebe, m. Capt. Frederick William Callahan.

Hanley, Capt. Matthew. At North-Kingston, Capt. M. H. to Miss Lydia Pettis. (W. Oct. 8, 1794.)

Harback, Sally, m. James Symmes.

Harden, Joanna, m. Samuel Watts.

Harding, Jane, m. Rev. Thomas Henley Chipman.

Harding, Martha, m. Richard Richardson.

Harmond, Polly; m. Thomas Stepson.

Harrington, Anna, m. Thomas Winship.

Harris, Hannah, m. William Draper.

Harris, J. E. In England, J. E. Harris, Esq., to Miss Joanna Hutchinson, daughter of the late Gov. Hutchinson of this State. (S. July 15, 1786.)

Harris, Joanna, m. Isaac Pierce.

Harris, Joseph. Last Tuesday evening, by the Rev. Mr. Stillman, Mr. J. H. to Miss Polly Daniels, both of this town. (S. Aug. 27, 1791.)

Harris, Lydia Gilbert, m. George Singleton, jun.

Harris, Rebeccah, m. Dr. John Wheeler.

Harris, Thankful, m. Jeremiah Gore, jun.

Harris, Rev. William. At Lexington, the Rev. W. H., of Marblehead, to Miss Patty Clark, daughter to the Rev. Mr. Clark, of Lexington. (S. Nov. 26, 1791.)

Harrison, Miss, m. Capt. Thomas Beaty.

Harrison, Betsy, m. Snelling Powell.

Harrison, George. At Philadelphia, Mr. G. H. to Miss Sophia Francis, daughter to Tench Francis, Esq. (W. Feb. 29, 1792.)

Harrow, Anna Matilda, m. Jacobus Hatchet.

Hartwell, Joseph. In this town, Mr. J. H. to Miss Esther M'Clarey. (W. Sept. 14, 1791.)

Hartwick, Hannah, m. Josiah Allen, jun.

Haskel, Phineas, jun. At Westborough, Mr. P. H., jun., to Miss Sukey Martyn. (W. Dec. 19, 1792.)

Haskell, Ruth, m. Simeon Haskell.

Haskell, Simeon. At Brookfield, Mr. S. H. to Miss Ruth Haskell, daughter of Mr. Samuel Haskell, D.D. (W. Dec. 4, 1793.)

Haskins, Deborah, m. Rev. Mase Shephard.

Haskins, Mary, m. William Ladd, jun.

Haskins, William. [At New-Bedford] Mr. W. H. to Miss Sally Potter. (W. Oct. 23, 1793.)

Hastings, John. At Newton, J. H., Esq., to the amiable Miss Sally Gardner, of Brooklyn. (W. Oct. 5, 1791.)

Hastings, Simon. In this town, last Thursday evening, by the Rev. Mr. Kirkland, Mr. S. H. to Miss Mindwell Andrews. (S. Nov. 22, 1794.)

Hatch, Asa. In this town, Mr. A. H. to Miss Patty Brown. (W. July 30, 1794.)

Hatch, Crowel. C. H., Esq., to Miss Hannah Boit. [Both of this town.] (W. Sept. 30, 1789.)

Hatch, Elizabeth, m. Samuel Quincey.

Hatch, Mrs. Phebe, m. Henry Sweetser.

Hatchet, Jacobus. [In this town] Mr. J. H. to Miss Anna Matilda Harrow. (W. Nov. 26, 1794.)

Hathaway, John. In this town, Mr. J. H. to Miss Hannah Tate. (W. May 16, 1792.)

Hathaway, Lydia, m. Caleb Faxon.

Hathaway, Nabby, m. Capt. Weston Howland.

Hathorne, Betsey, m. Thorndike Proctor, jun.

Hawes, Betsy, m. Capt. Benjamin Walcutt.

Hawes, Daniel. At Wrentham, Mr. D. H. to Miss Jemima Cheever. (S. Feb. 28, 1789.)

Hawkins, John. At Nantucket, Mr. J. H. to Miss Lucinda Whippy. (W. July 17, 1793.)

Hawks, Benjamin. At Salem, Mr. B. H. to Miss Nabby Becket. (S. Sept. 3, 1791.)

Hawson, Mrs. Margaret, m. Christopher Wilder.

Hayden, Capt. Caleb. In this town, Capt. C. H. to the agreeable Miss Caroline Stevens, both of this town. (W. June 15, 1791.)

Hayden, Eli. At Braintree, by the Rev. Mr. Wild, Mr. E. H. to Miss Charlotte Soper, both of that town. (S. Feb. 7, 1789.)

Hayden, Lot. Mr. L. H. to Miss Nancy Colesworthy. (W. June 30, 1790.)

Hayden, William. [In this town] Mr. W. H., of Richmond (Virg.), to Miss Lucy Davis, daughter of Mr. Edward Davis. (S. Oct. 13, 1792.)

Hayley, Mrs. Mary, m. Patrick Jeffrey.

Hayt, Monson. At Jamaica, M. H., Esq., to Miss Lucretia Hamersley. (S. Apr. 28, 1792.)

Hayward, Sally, m. Caleb Alden.

Hayward, Dr. Samuel. Dr. S. H., of this town, to the amiable Miss Sally Henshaw, of Connecticut.

Palma velut, palmam cui casta columba columbum
Sic vero conjux conjugem amore colat,
Conjugium fæcundat amor atq secundat,
Ditatidem Cœlo gratia lapsa dei.

ENGLISHED.

As hand with hand, as dove unites with dove,
Those link'd in wedlock, should be link'd in love,
Love join'd with labour should compleat the state,
And make that lasting which before was great,
When such fruition to terrestriars given,
Who would not wish for marriage in Heaven?
Or who thus blest, would wish to enter there?
Wedlock's a Heav'n beyond what angels share.

Hazeltine, Nancy, m. Daniel Stockwell.

Heacock, Theodora, m. Capt. Gilbert Horny.

Head, Ann, m. Phillip Jarvis.

Heard, Sally, m. Vashai Heminway.

Hearsey, Abel. At Salem, Mr. A. H. to Miss Polly Gardner. (W. Sept. 18, 1793.)

Hearsy, Thomas. In this town, Mr. T. H. to Miss Nancy Ayers. (S. Apr. 2, 1791.)

Heartshorn, Pliny. Mr. P. H. to Miss Sally Daniels [both] of this town. (W. Oct. 15, 1794.)
On Sunday evening last?

Heath, Ebenezer. At Roxbury, Mr. E. H., of Brooklyn, to the amiable Miss Hannah Williams, of Roxbury. (W. Jan. 12, 1791.)

Heath, William. In this town, by the Rev. Mr. Belknap, Mr. W. H. to Miss Betsy Black. (S. Mar. 6, 1790.)

Hedge, B., jun. At Fairfield, in Mr. Burr's house, Mr. B. H., jun., to Miss Eunice D. Burr, Mr. W. H. Capers, of S. Carolina, to Miss Abigail Burr, — and Mr. Gershom Burr to Miss Young. (W. Sept. 16, 1789.)

Heminway, Vashai. At Lancaster, Mr. V. H., of Shrewsbury, to Miss Sally Heard, daughter to Col. Heard, of Lancaster. (W. Feb. 15, 1792.)

Henderson, Joseph, m. Dr. William Cutler.

Henderson, Dr. R. At Staten Island, Dr. R. H. to Miss Maria Journeay. (W. May 16, 1792.)

Henry, Mrs. Elizabeth, m. Capt. Joseph Roby.

Henry, Jane, m. Capt. J. Gay.

Henshaw, Capt. Joshua. By the Rev. Dr. Lathrop, on Monday evening, Capt. J. H. to Miss Cynthia Lapham. (W. Feb. 2, 1791.)

Henshaw, Sally, m. Dr. Samuel Hayward.

Herring, Betsy, m. William Leggett.

Hewes, Elizabeth, m. Major John Gardner.

Hewes, Hannah, m. J. Deverell.

Hewes, Lucretia, m. William T. Clap.

Heyer, Eliza, m. Edward Meeks.

Heyler, Polly, m. Samuel Thaxter.

Hichborn, Betsy, m. Doddridge Crocker.

Hichborn, John. [In this town] Mr. J. H. to Miss Betsy Brown, daughter to Mr. Garven Brown. (S. Oct. 1, 1791.)

Hichborn, Phillip. In this town, Mr. P. H. to Miss Betsy Hopkins. (W. Sept. 19, 1792.)

Hichborn, Samuel. On Sunday evening, by the Rev. Mr. Parker, Mr. S. H. to the amiable Miss Nancy Rumsey. (W. Feb. 16, 1785.)

Hickey, Mrs. Betsy, m. Richard Champney.

Hicklin, Catharine, m. William Prescott.

Hickling, Elizabeth Parker, m. Gamaliel Bradford, jun.

Hicks, Willet. [At New York] Mr. W. H. to Miss Mary Matlack. (S. May 19, 1792.)

Hidden, Martha, m. Joseph Kilborn.

Hiestrine, Miss, m. Capt. Benjamin Hodgdon.

Higgins, Jane, m. Methusela Baldwin.

Higgins, Mercy, m. David Spear, jun.

Higginson, Nathaniel Cabot. At Philadelphia, N. C. H., Esq., to Miss Sally Rhea. (W. Oct. 24, 1792.)

Higginson, Sally, m. Dudley Atkins Tyng.

Higginson, Hon. Stephen. Hon. S. H., Esq., to Miss Elizabeth Perkins. (S. June 27, 1789.)

Higginson, Hon. Stephen. In this town, Hon. S. H., Esq., to Miss Sally Perkins. (W. Nov. 7, 1792.)

Hilegas, Miss, m. William Nickles.

Hill, Mrs. Charlotte, m. Capt. Joseph Gleason.

Hill, David. [In this town] Mr. D. H. to Miss Lydia Barron. (W. Apr. 3, 1793.)

Hill, Hannah, m. Samuel Whiting.

Hill, James. At Stockbridge, Mr. J. H., printer, late of this town, to Miss Jerusha Gardner. (S. Oct. 4, 1794.)

Hill, Sally, m. John Hunting.

Hill, Samuel. Mr. S. H. to Miss Grace Austin. (W. May 11, 1791.)

Hill, William. Mr. W. H. to Miss Polly Green. (W. Apr. 7, 1790.)

Hiller, Thomas. [In this town] Mr. T. H. to Miss Katy Martin. (S. Jan. 19, 1793.)

Hilton, Thomas. [At Portland] Mr. T. H. to Miss Rachel Veasie. (S. Nov. 26, 1791.)

Hinds, John. [In this town] Mr. J. H. to Miss Elizabeth Cotton. (S. Apr. 5, 1794.)

Hinkley, Hannah, m. Foster Crafts.

Hinkley, Sally, m. Watson Freeman.

Hinkley, Samuel. [At Northampton] S. H. to Miss Dorothy Strong. (W. June 28, 1786.)

Hitchcock, Joseph. [At New York] Mr. J. H. to Miss Sally Van Deuser. (S. Feb. 2, 1793.)

Hitchins, Sukey, m. Nathaniel Emmons.

Hixon, Mrs., m. Mr. Eaton.

Hobart, Racheal, m. Jothan Cushman.

Hodgdon, Capt. Benjamin. [At Philadelphia] Capt. B. H., formerly of this town, to the amiable Miss Hiestrine, of that city. (S. Jan. 7, 1792.)

Hodgdon, Nancy, m. William Keer.

Hodge, Hannah, m. Abiel Wood, jun.

Hodge, Sukey, m. Mr. Kennedy.

Hodges, Jonathan. [At Salem] Mr. J. H. to Miss Betsey Roper. (S. Apr. 5, 1788.)

Hodges, Thomas. [At Portland] Mr. T. H., merchant, of London, to Miss Jane Robinson. (S. July 23, 1790.)

Hoffman, Mary, m. James Seton.

Holbrook, Dr. [At Milton] Dr. H. to Miss Robinson, daughter to the late Col. Robinson, of Dorchester, deceased. (W. Dec. 9, 1789.)

Holland, Abial, m. Stephen Veron.

Holland, Mrs. Mary, m. Capt. David Spear.

Hollis, Mrs. Mary. [In this town] Mrs. M. H., aged 40,

to Master Benjamin Hooten, aged 18. (S. Jan. 19, 1793.

Hollister, William. [At Lenox] Mr. W. H. to Miss Orra Willard. (W. Nov. 17, 1790.)

Holman, Polly, m. Josiah Copeland.

Holmes, Betsy, m. Daniel Scott.

Holt, Polly, m. John Foster.

Holt, Sally, m. Joseph Brown.

Homans, Capt. Benjamin. [In this town] Capt. B. H. to Miss Martha Newell [both] of this town. (W. Aug. 3, 1791.)

Homans, Dr. John. Dr. J. H. to Miss Sally Dalton, both of this town. (S. Sept. 17, 1785.)

Homans, Susannah, m. Peter C. Scott.

Homer, Abiah, m. John Bonner.

Homer, Bethiah, m. Col. Oliver Gallup.

Homer, Betsey, m. Amasa Paine.

Homer, Mrs. Betsey, m. John Winnek.

Homer, Eleazer. Mr. E. H. to Miss Polly Bartlett. (S. Nov. 25, 1786.)

Homer, George. [In this town] Mr. G. H. to Miss Sally Sumner. (W. Nov. 30, 1791.)

Homer, Hannah, m. John Howe.

Homer, Capt. Michael. In this town, by the Rev. Mr. Thatcher, Capt. M. H. to Miss Betsey Rea, both of this town. (W. Nov. 16, 1791.)

Homer, Ruth, m. Peter Remy Arsonneau.

Homer, Sally, m. Samuel Dashwood.

Homes, Barzillia. [In this town] Mr. B. H. to Miss Sally Wheeler [both] of this town. (S. Dec. 15, 1792.)

Homes, Samuel. At the Rev. Mr. Porter's meeting-house, in the North Parish in Bridgewater, on Sunday last, after the public exercise was past, Mr. S. H. to the amiable Miss Polly Alcott. (S. Jan. 11, 1794.)

Homes, William. In this town, Mr. W. H. to Miss Mary Greenough. (W. Jan. 15, 1794.)

Hooper, Joseph. At Bridgewater, Mr. J. H. to Miss Lucy Mitchell, daughter of Mr. Edward Mitchell, of that town. (S. Jan. 5, 1793.)

Hooper, Joshua. At Charlestown, by the Rev. Mr. Morse,

Mr. J. H. to the amiable Miss Hannah Barrington, both of Charlestown. (W. July 24, 1793.)

Methinks the bliss must be complete,
Where wit and beauty jointly meet;
More pleasing still the nuptial bands,
Where honor, virtue, join their hands.

Hooper, Louise, m. Samuel Woodward.
Hooper, Ruth, m. Lewis Jenkins.
Hooper, Thomas. At Newburyport, Mr. T. H. to Miss Harriet Bradbury, of that town. (W. Sept. 26, 1792.)
Hooten, Benjamin, m. Mrs. Mary Hollis.
Hopkins, Miss, m. Joseph James.
Hopkins, Betsy, m. Phillip Hichborn.
Hopkins, Betsey, m. Leonard Worcester.
Hopkins, John. In Virginia, J. H., Esq., Continental Loan Officer, to Miss Lyons. (S. Nov. 7, 1789.)
Hopkins, Mary, m. Ashbel Wells.
Hopkins, Susannah, m. Rev. Jonathan Maxcy.
Hoppin, Col. Benjamin. At Warwick, Col. B. H., of Providence, to Mrs. Mary Whitney, of the former place. (W. June 18, 1794.)
Horn, Nancy, m. Hezekiah Hudson.
Horny, Capt. Gilbert. At Portsmouth, N. H., Capt. G. H., of Pool, in England, to Miss Theodore Heacock, of Cork, in Ireland. (W. Mar. 28, 1792.)
Houghton, Charity, m. Isaac Smith.
Houghton, Maverick, m. Dr. Josiah Cotting.
Hovey, Sally, m. Stephen Field.
Hovey, Sally, m. Daniel Jenkins, jun.
How, Rachel, m. Lieut. Edward Robinson.
How, Sally, m. Edmund Baker.
Howard, Rev. Dr. At Hingham, on Monday evening last, the Rev. Dr. H. to the agreeable Miss Jerusha Gay, daughter of the late Rev. Dr. Gay. (S. Dec. 4, 1790.)
M., 29 Nov., Rev. Simeon Howard, of Boston.
Howard, Abigail, m. Daniel Lincoln.
Howard, Amasa. At Westminster (Vt.), A. H., Esq., attorney-at-law, to Miss Betsy Homer, second daughter of the late Capt. Benjamin Homer, deceased, of this town. (W. Sept. 12, 1787.)

Howard, Rev. Bezaleel. At Weathersfield (Conn.), the Rev. B. H., of Springfield, to Miss Prudence Williams. (W. May 26, 1790.)

Howard, Eliza, m. Samuel Phipps.

Howard, Dr. John. At Moriches, Suffolk County, Dr. J. H. to Miss Fanny Howell.

Howard, Judith, m. Capt. Joseph Clark.

Howard, Mary, m. M. Bussy.

Howe, Hipzabath, m. Jacob Barnes.

Howe, John. Mr. J. H. to Miss Hannah Homer. In this town implied. (S. Dec. 28, 1793.)

Howe, Joseph. In this town, Mr. J. H. to Miss Patty Gridley, both of this town. (W. Sept. 17, 1794.)

Howe, Maria, m. John Coates.

Howe, Polly, m. Robert Crocker.

Howe, Polly, m. Hawks Lincoln.

Howe, Thomas. Mr. T. H. to Miss Alice Sumner. (W. Mar. 9, 1791.)

Howe, Thomas. [In this town] Mr. T. H. to Miss Ann Gardner. (W. June 6, 1792.)

Howell, Fanny, m. Dr. John Howard.

Howell, Dr. Jeremiah B. At Providence, Dr. J. B. H. to Miss Martha Brown, daughter of the late Mr. J. B. (S. E.) (W. Oct. 30, 1793.)

Howes, William. [At Warren] Mr. W. H., of Wrentham, to Miss Eunice Dagget, of Attleborough. (S. Nov. 23, 1793.)

Howland, Alice, m. Jarathmael White.

Howland, Beriah. At Dartmouth, Mr. B. H., of Westport, to Mr. Lucy Brightman of New-Bedford. (S. Dec. 15, 1792.)

Howland, Hannah, m. Capt. William Akin.

Howland, Capt. Weston. At New-Bedford, Capt. W. H. to Miss Nabby Hathaway. (W. Oct. 23, 1793.)

Hoy, Miss, m. Earl of Shrewsbury.

Hoyt, Dr. Benjamin Starr. At Danbury, Dr. B. S. H. to Miss Ann Wood. (W. Oct. 1, 1794.)

Hoyt, Dr. Ezra. At Lanesborough, Dr. E. H. to Miss Sally Smith, eldest daughter of Col. Jonathan Smith, the gentleman whose speech in Convention, "to his brother Farmers," was so much celebrated. (S. Mar. 20, 1790.)

Hubbard, John. At New-Ipswich, on the 10th inst., Mr. J. H., Preceptor of the New-Ipswich Academy, to Miss Becca Preston of New-Ipswich. (W. Aug. 24, 1791.)
Hudson, Hezekiah. [In this town] Mr. H. H. to Miss Nancy Horn. (W. Apr. 4, 1792.)
Hughes, Samuel, jun. [In this town] Mr. S. H., jun. to Miss Peggy Milliquet. (W. Oct. 26, 1791.)
Hull, Dr. David. At Fairfield, Conn., Dr. D. H. to Miss Sukey Eliot, daughter of the late Rev. Dr. Eliot, of this town. (S. Nov. 14, 1789.)
Humphrey, Betsey, m. Charles Leach.
Humphrey, Capt. James, jun. At Fitzwilliam, Capt. J. H., jun., of Athol, to Miss Lucy Brigham. (Dec. 25, 1793.)
Humphrey, Sukey, m. Samuel Fenner.
Hunnewell, Jonathan. Mr. J. H. to Miss Katy Gore, daughter of John Gore, Esq., of this town. (W. Dec. 5, 1787.)
Hunnewell, Sally, m. John W. Bradlee.
Hunt, Joab. [In this town] By the Rev. Dr. Parker, Mr. J. H. to Miss Kezia Wentworth, of this town. (W. Nov. 9, 1791.)
Hunt, Rebecca, m. Dr. Nathaniel Noyes.
Hunt, Samuel. [In this town] On Monday evening, Mr. S. H. to the amiable Mrs. Shepard, of South-Carolina. (W. May 5, 1790.)
Hunt, Samuel W. Last evening, Mr. S. W. H. to Miss Ruthy Mackay. (W. Oct. 18, 1786.)
Hunt, Thomas. Last evening, at Roxbury, by the Rev. Mr. Porter, Mr. T. H., of Stockbridge, to Miss Polly Patten, only daughter of Capt. Nathaniel Patten, of that place. (W. Oct. 28, 1789.)
Hunt, William. Thursday afternoon, by the Rev. S. Parker, W. H., Esq., of Watertown, attorney-at-law, to Miss Jenny Bethune, of Little Cambridge. (S. Nov. 17, 1787.)
Hunter, Anne, m. John L. T. D. Falconet.
Hunter, Peggy, m. Ebenezer Coombs.
Hunting, John. [In this town] Mr. J. H. to Miss Sally Hill. (W. Oct. 24, 1792.)

Huntington, Jabez. At Norwich, Mr. J. H., merchant, to Miss Mary Lanman. (W. Jan. 2, 1793.)

Hurten, Maria, m. Timothy Burr.

Hussey, Amelia, m. William Mackay, jun.

Hussey, Hon. Jethro. At Nantucket, the Hon. J. H., Esq., to Mrs. Margaret Snow. (S. Mar. 23, 1793.)

Hussey, Sally, m. Capt. Gersham Cox.

Hutchins, Miss, m. Captain M'Lane.

Hutchins, James R. At Menotomy, by the Rev. Mr. Fiske, Mr. J. R. H., printer, of Windsor, to Miss Marianne Thomas, only daughter of Isaiah Thomas, Esq., of Worcester. (W. Jan. 18, 1792.)

Hutchinson, Joanna, m. J. E. Harris.

Hynard, John Henry. Mr. J. H. H. to Miss Hannah Jennings. (S. June 18, 1785.)

Hyrne, Mrs. S., m. Benjamin C. Cutler.

Hyslop, David. At Concord, Mr. D. H., of Brooklyne, to Miss Eliza Stone. (S. Sept. 21, 1793.)

Hyslop, William, jun. On Monday evening last, at Lynn, Mr. W. H., jun., of this town, to Miss Betsey Williams, of Salem. (W. June 13, 1787.)

Ide, Lemuel. [At Shrewsbury] Mr. L. I. to Miss Sarah Stone. (W. Dec. 11, 1793.)
See also Lewis Keyes.

Ingalls, Miss, m. Capt. Manassah Marston.

Ingersol, Capt. Jonathan. At Salem, Capt. J. I. to Miss Mary Poole. (S. Feb. 16, 1793.)

Ingersol, Mary, m. Samuel Leeds, jun.

Ingersol, Sarah, m. Samuel Prince.

Ingersoll, Nabby, m. David Peirce.

Inglesly, Polly, m. Michael Malony.

Inglish, Priscilla, m. Richard W. Cooper.

Ingraham, Capt. Joseph. Capt. J. I. to Miss Jenny Salter, daughter of Mr. Richard Salter. (S. Oct. 15, 1785.)

Innes, Hon. Henry. At Danville (Ken.), Hon. H. I., Esq., to Mrs. Shields. (W. Apr. 18, 1792.)

Ireland, John. At Cambridge, Mr. J. I. to the amiable Miss Hannah Philips, both of that place. (W. May 21, 1794.)

Irish, Sally, m. William Baily.

Irving William, jun. At Philadelphia, Mr. W. I., jun., to Miss Julia Paulding, of Greenbourg. (W. Nov. 20, 1793.)

Ivers, Elizabeth, m. William Cleland.

Ivers, Jane, m. Benjamin Austin, jun.

Ivers, Mrs. Mary, m. John Sprague.

Ivers, Nancy, m. Oliver Brewster.

Ivers, Thomas P. At Providence, Mr. T. P. I. to the amiable Miss Hope Brown, daughter of the late Nicholas Brown, Esq., a lady of great fortune. On this happy occasion, the elegant chandelier in the Baptist meeting-house was lighted by the Society, as well to testify their joy on the auspicious event as to evince their grateful sensibility to the young lady for her truly generous donation to the Society, by which the sacred temple is so richly and beautifully embellished. (W. Mar. 14, 1792.)

Jackson, Charles. At Plymouth, Mr. C. J. to Miss Lucy Cotten. (S. Mar. 15, 1794.)

Jackson, Elizabeth, m. Capt. Nathan G. Thompson.

Jackson, John. In this town, Mr. J. J. to Mrs. —— Avery [both of this town]. (W. Aug. 3, 1791.)

Jackson, Nabby, m. William Crombie, jun.

Jackson, Polly, m. William Ellison, jun.

Jackson, Thomas. At Plymouth, Mr. T. J., tert., to the amiable Miss Sally May. (S. Jan. 12, 1788.)

Jacobs, Sally, m. Stephen Hall.

Jacobs, Mrs. Sarah, m. Calvin Bailey.

James, Joseph. At Philadelphia, Mr. J. J., printer, to Miss Hopkins. (S. Oct. 1, 1791.)

James, Sally, m. Richard Gridley, jun.

Janes, Samuel. In this town, by the Rev. Dr. Howard, Mr. S. J., merchant, to Miss Lucretia Fiske, of Watertown. (S. Nov. 19, 1791.)

Jansen, Margaret, m. John Wyncoop.

Jarvis, John. Mr. J. J. to Miss Hannah Seabury. (S. Apr. 12, 1788.)

Jarvis, Phillip. In this town, last Sunday evening, Mr. P. J. to Miss Ann Head, eldest daughter of the late Mr. John Head, merchant. (S. Nov. 25, 1786.)

Jasper, Polly, m. John Dyer.

Jeffers, Capt. Samuel. At Newport, R. I., Capt. S. J. to Miss Betsy Drew, youngest daughter of the late Capt. James Drew. (W. Apr. 4, 1792.)

Jeffrey, Patrick. Mr. P. J. to Mrs. Mary Hayley. (W. June 14, 1786.)

Jenckes, Capt. John. At Providence, Capt. J. J. to Miss Elizabeth Cushing. (S. Nov. 9, 1793.)

Jenkins, Daniel, jun. Mr. D. J., jun., of Scituate, to Miss Sally Hovey, of this town. (W. Mar. 31, 1790.)

Jenkins, Lewis. At Newbury-Port, Mr. L. J., merchant, to Miss Ruth Hooper. (S. July 9, 1791.)

Jenks, Joseph. At Salem, Mr. J. J., merchant, to Miss Patty Abbot. (S. Sept. 6, 1788.)

Jenks, Mrs. Roby, m. Amos Reed.

Jennes, Polly, m. Rev. Jesse Remington.

Jennings, Daniel. Mr. D. J. to Miss Isabella Collins. (W. Feb. 17, 1790.)

Jennings, Hannah, m. John Henry Hynard.

Jennings, Margaret, m. Stoddard Capen.

Jennison, Ebenezer. Mr. E. J. to Miss Sally Webb [both of this town]. (S. Aug. 6, 1791.)

Jennison, Dr. J. At Cambridge, Dr. J. J. to the amiable Miss Belcher, daughter of his late Excellency Governor Belcher, of Nova Scotia, and granddaughter of his Excellency Jonathan Belcher, Esq., deceased, formerly Governor of the provinces of Massachusetts Bay and New Hampshire. (S. Aug. 28, 1790.)

Jewitt, Mrs., m. Larkin Thorndike.

Johnson, Coffin. [At Newburyport] Mr. C. J. to Miss Sally Avery. (S. Nov. 1, 1794.)

Johnson, George. At Philadelphia, G. J. Esq., of Annapolis, to Miss Van Deren, of Philadelphia. (W. May 16, 1792.)

Johnson, George. [In this town] Mr. G. J. to Miss Olive Body. (S. Sept. 27, 1794.)

Johnson, Hannah, m. Samuel Totman.

Johnson, Joel. In this town, Mr. J. J. to Miss Polly Sibley. (S. Apr. 5, 1794.)

Johnson, Micajah. [At Salem] Mr. M. J. to Miss Sally Berry. (S. Sept. 3, 1791.)

Johnson, Ruth, m. David Morse.

Johnson, Sally, m. John Soren.

Johnson, Samuel. At Providence, Mr. S. J. to Miss Nancy Gilmore, daughter of Mr. Nathaniel Gilmore. (S. Jan. 19, 1793.)

Johnson, Suckey, m. Thomas Leverett.

Johnson, William. Mr. W. J. to Miss Sally Adams. (W. Dec. 25, 1793.)

Johnston, John. [At New York] Mr. J. J. to Miss S. Bard. (W. June 13, 1792.)

Jones, Capt. Amassa. At Hartford, Capt. A. J., of that city, to Miss Cynthia Jones, of Adams. (S. May 19, 1792.)

Jones, Cynthia, m. Capt. Amassa Jones.

Jones, Ephraim. At Lincoln, Mr. E. J., of Concord, to Miss Lucy Phillips, daughter of Capt. Benjamin Phillips. (W. Jan. 3, 1787.)

Jones, Fanny, m. Joseph Allen.

Jones, Henry Charles. At New York, H. C. J., Esq., merchant, to Miss Amy Whipple Burroughs, of Providence. (W. Oct. 29, 1794.)

Jones, John. Mr. J. J., of Providence, to Miss Rebecca Burroughs. (W. Oct. 27, 1790.)

Jones, John Coffin. At Newport, J. C. J., Esq., of this town, to Miss Abigail Grant, daughter of the late Alexander Grant, Esq. (W. May 24, 1786.)

Jones, John Coffin. At Newport, J. C. J., Esq., of this town, to the amiable Miss Elizabeth Champlin, daughter to Christopher Champlin, Esq., of that place. (Sept. 14, 1791.)

Jones, Joseph. [In this town] Mr. J. J. to Miss Susannah Farn, both of this town. (W. Aug. 27, 1794.)

Jones, Katharine, m. Capt. William Brown.

Jones, Nancy, m. Oswald Lombart.

Jones, Polly, m. Adonijah Stevens.

Jones, Polly, m. William Wheeler.

Jones, Rowland. At Portland, Mr. R. J. to Miss Polly Godson. (S. Feb. 11, 1792.)

Jones, Theodore. At No. 4, Union-River, Mr. T. J. to Miss Catharine Sargent, daughter of Paul Sargent, Esq., of Frenchman's Bay, town of Sullivan, in the County of Han-

Jones, William. At Concord, Mr. W. J., of this town, to Miss Rhoda Soper, of that place. (W. Apr. 28, 1790.)

Jordan, Elizabeth, m. John Pitcher.

Jorden, Capt. Tristram. At Kittery, Capt. T. J., of Biddeford, to Miss Polly Fernald. (S. Oct. 17, 1789.)

Jordis, Frederick. At Salem, Mr. F. J. to Miss Anne Long. (W. Dec. 24, 1794.)

Journeay, Maria, m. Dr. R. Henderson.

Joy, Jedidiah. Mr. J. J., of Hingham, to Miss Fanny Ranger, of Hull. (S. Aug. 8, 1789.)

Judal, Sally, m. Samuel Myers.

Justin, Philip. [At Newport] Mr. P. J., of Providence, to Miss Bessie Knapp. (S. Nov. 5, 1794.)

Jutau, John. Last Sunday evening, by the Rev. Mr. Parker, Mr. J. J. to Mrs. Polly Premir. (W. Aug. 30, 1786.)

Kahleer, Jeremiah. In this town, by the Rev. Dr. Sullivan, Mr. J. K. to Miss Hannah Spear. (War. Mar. 12, 1794.)

Kammerer, Miss, m. Isaac Neale.

Keen, Joseph. At Kittery, Mr. J. K. to Miss Hannah Bernard. (S. Nov. 22, 1794.)

Keer, William. [In this town] Mr. W. K. to Miss Nancy Hodgdon. (W. July 16, 1794.)

Kellog, Rev. Elijah. At Portland, Rev. E. K. to Miss Eunice M'Lellan. (W. July 18, 1792.)

Kelly, Rev. John. At Chester, the Rev. J. K., of Hampstead, to Miss Nabby Dearborn, daughter to Mr. John S. Dearborn, of Chester. (S. Aug. 24, 1793.)

Kemble, T. H. In this town, on Sunday week last, by the Rev. Dr. Eckley, Mr. T. H. K., merchant, to the amiable Miss Abigal Bumstead, only daughter of Maj. Thomas Bumstead. (W. Aug. 27, 1794.)

Kendall, Miss, m. Joseph Anderson.

Kendall, Lucey, m. Stephen Lamson.

Kendall, Rev. Samuel. At Weston, the Rev. S. K. to Miss Nabby Woodward, eldest daughter of his predecessor, the Rev. Samuel Woodward. (W. Oct. 25, 1786.)

Kennedy, Mr. [At Wiscasset] Mr. K. to Miss Sukey Hodge. (W. Jan. 8, 1794.)

Kennedy, John. Mr. J. K., merchant, to Miss Sally Hall, daughter of Mr. Isaac Hall. (S. Nov. 2, 1893.)

Kenney, Samuel. In this town, Mr. S. K. to Miss Mary Field. (W. Oct. 27, 1790.)

Kenny, Jesse. [At Salem] Mr. J. K. to Miss Hannah Mascoll. (W. Jan. 23, 1793.)

Kent, Maj. Ebenezer. In this town, Maj. E. K. of Watertown, to Miss Charlotte Vinall, daughter of John Vinall, Esq., of this town. (W. Sept. 3, 1794.)

Kent, Huldah, m. Israel Evans.

Kent, William A. At Hanover, Mr. W. A. K., of New Concord, merchant, to Miss Charlotte Mellen, daughter to the Rev. John Mellen, of that place. (W. May 9, 1792.)

Kerr, Agnes, m. William Wilson.

Kettle, James. At Portland, Mr. J. K. to Miss Polly Quincy. (W. Apr. 25, 1792.)

Kettle, John. Mr. J. K. to Miss Suckey Frothingham, both of this town. (S. Aug. 2, 1786.)

Kettle, John. At Salem, Mr. J. K., of Danvers, to Mrs. Ann Smith, of Beverly. (W. Nov. 19, 1794.)

Key, Edward. At Pottsgrave, Penn., E. K., Esq., to Miss Anna Potts. (S. July 14, 1792.)

Keyes, Lewis. At Shrewsbury, Mr. L. K. to Miss Sarah Stone, Mr. Lemuel Ide to Miss Sarah Stone, daughters of Messrs. Joseph and Jasper Stone. (W. Dec. 11, 1793.)

Kidder, Betsey, m. Benjamin Raymond.

Kidder, Phebe, m. Nathaniel Leach.

Kilborn, Joseph. At Rowley, Mr. J. K., aged 75, to Miss Martha Hidden, aged 26.

"Strange that desire should so long outlive performance."

Shakespeare.

Kilton, Wait, m. Joshua Rathbon.

Kilty, Capt. John. At Annapolis, Capt. J. K. to Miss Quynn. (S. May 26, 1792.)

Kimball, Hannah, m. Caleb Bingham.

Kimball, Jesse. At Hallowell, Mr. J. K. to Miss Hannah Cox. (W. Dec. 31, 1794.)

Kimball, Sukey, m. Isaac Long.

Kimble, Joseph A. Mr. J. A. K. to Miss Patty Redman. (W. Oct. 5, 1791.)

King, George. At Patchog (Long-Island), Mr. G. K., aged

36, to Sally King, aged 12 years and 2 months. (W. Dec. 12, 1792.)

King, Jared. At Kingston (Y)., Mr. J. K., æt. 19, to Miss Polly Dean, æt. 12. At Lanesborough, in this State, Dea. Jacob Burgin, æt. 81, to Mrs. Elizabeth Weed, æt. 63. (S. Nov. 23, 1793.)

☞ *After reading these two articles, who shall say that Love is not blind!*

King, Polly, m. Capt. George Lane.

King, Sally, m. George King.

Kingsbury, Nathaniel. By the Rev. Mr. Eckley, Mr. N. K. to Miss Ruth Norris, both of this town. (S. Jan. 7, 1892.)

Kingsbury, Rev. Mr. [At Longmeadow] Rev. Mr. K. to Miss Polly Reynolds. (W. Feb. 22, 1792.)
See also Rev. Mr. Bascom.

Kinsley, Timothy. At Lebanon, Mr. T. K. to Miss Sybil Fisk. (S. April 14, 1792.)

Kinsman, Hannah, m. William Paine.

Kip, Isaac L. At New York, I. L. K., Esq., attorney at law, to Miss Sarah Smith. (S. March 10, 1792.)

Kirk, George. At New York, Mr. G. K. to Miss Nancy Wright. (W. April 18, 1792.)

Kirkwood, Elizabeth, m. Paul Rolfe.

Knap, Anne, m. Nathaniel Cobb.

Knapp, Betsey, m. Philip Justin.

Knapp, John. At Philadelphia, Mrs. J. K. to Miss Mary Phille. (S. Sept. 8, 1792.)

Knapp, John, jun. [At Newburyport] Mr. J. K., jun., to Miss Mary Davis. (S. Nov. 1, 1794.)

Kneeland, Deborah, m. Samuel Dunnels.

Knickabacker, Rebecca, m. John Bradshaw.

Knight, Capt. Christopher. At Scituate, Capt. C. K., of Cranston, to Barbary Fisk, daughter of Peleg Fisk, Esq. (S. Dec. 28, 1793.)

Knight, Capt. Reuben. Capt. R. K. to Mrs. Sally Brown. (W. Dec. 9, 1789.)

Knowlton, Mrs., m. Dea. Joseph Allen.

Knox, Barnabas. In this town, Mr. B. K. to Miss Rachel Tilton. (W. June 19, 1793.)

Knox, Capt. Thomas. [In this town] Capt. T. K. to Miss Ruthy Eliot. (S. Oct. 13, 1792.)

Kuhu, Jacob. Mr. J. K. to Miss Hannah Frost. (W. Oct. 13, 1790.)

Kumbel, Elizabeth, m. Capt. John H. Shackerly.

Lackay, Mrs., m. John Chicken.

Ladd, Elizabeth, m. Dr. John Haskins.

Ladd, William, jun. Mr. W. L., jun., to Miss Mary Haskins, both of this town. (S. Nov. 9, 1793.)

Laha, Marcy, m. John Fox.

Lamb, Deziah, m. Samuel Clap.

Lambert, Caleb. [At Bath, Kennebeck] Mr. C. L. to Miss Lucy Benny. (W. Nov. 12, 1794.)

Lambert, Polly, m. Samuel Sewall.

Lampson, Isaac. Mr. I. L. to Miss Abigail Fiske. (S. Dec. 27, 1788.)

Lamson, Caleb. At Charlestown, by the Rev. Mr. Morse, Mr. C. L. to Miss Joanna Rand. (S. Mar. 1, 1794.)

Lamson, Mrs. Hannah, m. William Cogswell.

Lamson, Samuel. In this town, Mr. S. L. to Miss Thankful Eaton. (W. Dec. 3, 1794.)

Lamson, Stephen. At Ipswich, Mr. S. L. to Miss Lucey Kendall. (S. Aug. 31, 1793.)

Lander, Jonathan. Mr. J. L. to Miss Sally Warren, daughter of Capt. Benjamin Warren. (W. May 19, 1787.)

Lane, Cornelius. At Great Barrington, Mr. C. L. to Miss Nancy Oles. (S. March 2, 1793.)

Lane, Capt. George. Last Thursday evening, Capt. G. L. to Miss Polly King, a young lady truly amiable. (S. Jan. 21, 1786.)

See also Bridgman's King's Chapel inscr., pp. 129, 234.

Langdon, Henry S. [In this town] On Tuesday last, H. S. L., Esq., of Portsmouth, to Miss Nancy Eustis, of this town. (S. May 12, 1792.)

Langdon, John Wally. At Charlestown, on Tuesday evening last, Mr. J. W. L., merchant, to the amiable Miss Rebecca Cordis, daughter of Joseph Cordis, Esq., of that town. (S. Aug. 30, 1794.)

Langley, John, jun. At Newport, Mr. J. L., jun., to Miss Betsey Billings. (S. Nov. 17, 1792.)

Langley, Nabby, m. Isaac Greenwood.

Langoon, Elizabeth, m. Hon. David Sewall.

Langshaw, M., m. William Grace.

Lanier, Patsy, m. Mr. Mark.

Lanman, Mary, m. Jabez Huntington.

Lapham, Asa. Mr. A. L., of Marshfield, to Mrs. Dorcas Frost, of this town. (S. May 1, 1790.)

Lapham, Cynthia, m. Capt. Joshua Henshaw.

Larkin, Ebenezer, jun. [In this town] Mr. E. L., jun., to Miss Sukey Makepeace. (W. Dec. 26, 1792.)

Larkin, Isaac. In this town, on Thursday evening, Mr. I. L., printer, and Jun. Editor of the Chronicle, to Miss Nabby Clark. (S. Aug. 2, 1794.)

Larkin, Polly, m. Thomas Rand.

Larkin, Ruthy, m. Amariah Childs.

Larkin, Ruthy, m. Phillips Payson, jun.

Larkin, Sally, m. John Sargeant.

Larned, Darius. At Pittsfield, Mr. D. L. to Miss Eunice Marsh. (W. Nov. 17, 1790.)

Lathrop, Charles. At New-Canaan, C. L., Esq., to Miss Joanna Leffingwell. (S. May 4, 1793.)

Lathrop, Daniel. At Norwich, Mr. D. L., merchant, to Miss Betsey Turner. (S. Aug. 24, 1793.)

Lathrop, John, jun. In this town, Mr. J. L., jun., to Miss Ann Peirce, daughter of Mr. Joseph Pierce, merchant. (S. Apr. 27, 1793.)

Lathrop, Polly, m. Samuel Pierce.

Laughton, Elizabeth, m. Joseph Callender.

Laugier, J. H., Baron de Taffy. Last evening, Mr. J. H. L., Baron de Taffy, to Miss Hannah Minot, second daughter of Mr. Samuel Minot, of this town. (W. Dec. 3, 1788.)

Laurence, John A. At Connecticut, Mr. J. A. L., merchant, to Miss Sally Prentiss. (S. Mar. 31, 1792.)

Lawrence, Rev. Nathaniel. At Watertown, Rev. N. L., of Tingsbury, to Miss Hannah Soden, of Watertown. (W. May 28, 1794.)

Leach, Charles. At Weymouth, Mr. C. L., of this town, to Miss Betsey Humphrey, daughter of the Hon. James Humphrey, Esq. (S. Jan. 14, 1792.)

Leach, Nathaniel. Mr. W. L., of this town, to Miss Phebe Kidder, of Cambridge. (W. Mar. 7, 1787.)

Leach, Sally, m. Nathan Webb.

Leach, William. Mr. W. L. to Miss Betsey Swett. (S. Sept. 4, 1790.)

Lealand, Ebenezer. At Roxbury, Mr. E. L. to the amiable Mrs. Sukey Wilson. (S. Aug. 31, 1793.)

Lear, Tobias. At Portsmouth (N.H.), by the Rev. Dr. Haven, T. L., Esq., Secretary to the President of the United States, to Miss Polly Long, daughter of the late Hon. Peirce Long, Esq. (W. Apr. 28, 1790.)

> "Here Honour fair, shall bloom in manly youth,
> And Beauty's bosom prove the bed of Truth."

Leanord, Rev. Elijah. The Rev. E. L., of Marshfield, to Miss Mary Fobes, daughter of the Rev. Mr. Fobes, of Raynham. (S. May 19, 1792.)
Leonard?

Leathers, Phœbe, m. Francis Churchill.

Leathesby, James Holt. In this town, last evening, Mr. J. H. L. to Miss Rachel Williams, of Charlestown. (S. Aug. 18, 1792.)

Leavit, Hart. [At Deerfield] Mr. H. L., of Greenfield, to Miss Rachel Barnard. (S. Feb. 16, 1793.)
See also Capt. Joshua Clapp.

Leavitt, Elijah. In this town, Mr. E. L. to Miss Betsey Barry. (S. Feb. 15, 1794.)

Leavitt, Samuel. In Maine, Mr. S. L., of Buxton, to Miss Hannah Dearing, of Pepperelborough. (W. Dec. 25, 1793.)

Lee, Gov. In Virginia, His Excellency Gov. Lee to Miss Ann Carter. An event which promises the most auspicious fortune to the wedded pair. (S. July 6, 1793.)

Lee, Miss, m. J. Tremain, jun.

Lee, Ann, m. James Riley.

Lee, Hannah, m. Corban Washington.

Lee, Margaret, m. James Clark.

Lee, Richard Bland. At Germantown, R. B. L., Esq., one of the Members of Congress from Virginia, to Miss Collins, daughter of Mr. Stephen Collins, merchant, Philadelphia. (W. July 2, 1794.)

Lee, Susannah, m. Joseph Chapman.

Lee, Thomas. In Virginia, T. L., Esq., to Miss Mildred Washington, niece to Gen. Washington. (W. Nov. 26, 1788.)

Lee, William, jun. In this town, Mr. W. L., jun., to Miss Susan Palfrey. (S. June 28, 1794.)

Leeds, Patience, m. Enos Withington.

Leeds, Samuel, jun. At Dorchester, Mr. S. L., jun., to Miss Mary Ingersol. (W. June 5, 1793.)

Leffingwell, Hannah, m. Peleg Tracy.

Leffingwell, Joanna, m. Charles Lathrop.

Leggett, William. Mr. W. L. to Miss Betsey Herring. (S. May 8, 1790.)

Leitch, Sarah, m. John Addison.

Leonard, Dr. Boucher. At Malden, by the Rev. Mr. Willis, Dr. B. L., of Boston, to Miss Sarah Barrett, of Malden. (S. Jan. 3, 1789.)

Leonard, Oliver. At Newport, Mr. O. L. to Mrs. Sarah Fletcher. (S. March 5, 1791.)

Leroy, Herman. At New York, H. L., Esq., Consul from their High Mightinesses, to Miss Hannah Cornell, one of the daughters of the late Samuel Cornell, Esq., of Newbern, North Carolina. (S. Oct. 28, 1786.)

Leverett, Benjamin. At Portsmouth, Mr. B. L., merchant, to Miss Comfort Marshall. (S. July 10, 1790.)

Leverett, Hannah, m. John Leverett.

Leverett, John. In this town, Mr. J. L., merchant, of Windsor (Vt.), to Miss Hannah Leverett, of this town. (S. June 9, 1792.)

Leverett, Thomas. At Middletown, Mr. T. L., merchant, to Miss Suckey Johnson. (S. Nov. 20, 1790.)

Leverett, William. At Roxbury, Mr. W. L., merchant, of this town, to Miss Charlotte Whiting, daughter of Major Whiting, of that place. (W. Nov. 13, 1693.)

Levett, Abigail, m. Stephen Gulliver.

Lewis, Lathrop. At Gorham, Mr. L. L. to Miss Tabitha Longfellow. (S. Feb. 8, 1794.)

Lewis, Mary Ann, m. Nathaniel Gardner.

Lewis, Nabby, m. Samuel Austin.

Lewis, Robert. In Virginia, R. L., Esq. (nephew and Aide-de-Camp to the President of the U.S.), to Miss Brown. (S. May 7, 1794.)

Lewis, Roxa, m. John B. Darney.

Lewis, Thomas. In this town, Mr. T. L. to Miss Elizabeth Carpenter. (S. Jan. 4, 1794.)

Libbey, John. [At Portsmouth] Mr. J. L. to Miss Comfort Noble. (S. Nov. 22, 1794.)

Lillielbridge, Mr. In Georgia, Mr. L., aged 55, to Miss Osut, aged 17. (W. July 25, 1792.)

Lillie, Daniel, jun. In this town, Mr. D. L., jun., to Miss Nabby Cogswell. (W. Feb. 29, 1792.)

Lillie, John Sweetser. In this town, Mr. J. S. L. to Miss Sally Andrews. (S. May 12, 1792.)

Lillie, Sukey, m. Gamaliel Bradford.

Lillie, Thomas. By the Rev. John Elliot, Mr. T. L. to Miss Hannah Edes, both of this town. (S. Feb. 22, 1794.)

Lincoln, Abner. At Hingham, Mr. A. L., A.B., Preceptor of the Derby School in that town, to Miss Hannah Lincoln, daughter of the Hon. Benjamin Lincoln, Esq. (W. May 25, 1791.)

Lincoln, Daniel. By the Rev. Mr. Murray, Mr. D. L. to Miss Abigail Howard. (S. Nov. 30, 1793.)

Lincoln, David. At Roxbury, by the Rev. Mr. Porter, Mr. D. L. to Miss Lucy Tilton. (W. Nov. 27, 1793.)

Lincoln, Hannah, m. Abner Lincoln.

Lincoln, Hawks. In this town, Mr. H. L. to Miss Polly Howe. (S. July 6, 1793.)

Lincoln, Levi. At Hingham, Mr. L. L. to Miss Desire Thaxter. (W. Nov. 12, 1794.)

Lincoln, Capt. Michael. Capt. M. L., of Annapolis Royal, to Miss Hannah Stone, of this town. (W. Nov. 11, 1789.)

Lines, Ruthe, m. Noah Dogget.

Lions, Ann, m. Thomas Ross.

Lispenard, Helen, m. Paul R. Bache.

Lithgow, Arthur. At Pownalborough, A. L., Esq., to Miss Martha Bridge, daughter of Edmund Bridge, Esq., Sheriff of the County of Lincoln. (S. Jan. 1, 1791.)

Lithgow, Polly, m. James Davidson.

Little, Jane, m. Nathaniel Moody.

Little, Paul, jun. At Windham, Mr. P. L., jun., to Miss Polly Osgood. (S. May 12, 1792.)

Little, Persis, m. Rev. Allen Pratt.

Little, William. Mr. W. L. to Miss Frances Boyd, both of this town. (S. March 13, 1790.)

Littlejohn, Dr. Miles. At Baltimore, Dr. M. L. to Miss Sally Payne. (S. Oct. 13, 1792.)

Livermore, Mrs. Abigail, m. Amos Bond.

Livermore, Betsy, m. William Brown.

Livingston, Miss m. Marquiss Precee.

Livingston, John R. At New York, J. R. L., Esq., to Miss Eliza M'Evers, youngest daughter to Charles M'Evers, Esq. (W. June 10, 1789.)

Livingston, Peter W. At New York, P. W. L., Esq., to Miss Elizabeth Beekman. (W. Nov. 27, 1793.)

Livingston, Hon. Philip. At New York, the Hon. P. L., Esq., to Miss Cornelia Van Horne. (S. Oct. 30, 1790.)

Lloyd, Miss, m. Leonard Vassall Borland.

Lobdell, Mrs. Sally, m. John Pierce.

Locke, Edwin. In this town, Mr. E. L. to Miss Matilda Trask. (S. Sept. 20, 1794.)

Locke, Hitty, m. John Crosby.

Lombard, Daniel, jun. At Springfield, Mr. D. L., jun., of that town, to Miss Sylvia Burt, of Longmeadow. (W. Dec. 12, 1787.)

Lombart, Oswald. At Stockbridge, Mr. O. L., to Miss Nancy Jones of that town. (S. Nov. 14, 1789.)

Long, Anne, m. Frederick Jordis.

Long, Isaac. At Hopkinton, N.H., Mr. I. L., the celebrated architect, to Miss Sukey Kimball. (S. Jan. 11, 1794.)

Long, Polly,* m. Tobias Lear.

Longfellow, Tabitha, m. Lathrop Lewis.

Lopaus, John. Mr. J. L., of Charlestown, to Miss Hannah Tuckerman, of this town. (S. Sept. 5, 1789.)

Loring, Caleb. In this town, Mr. C. L. to Miss Nancy Greely. (S. Feb. 28, 1789.)

Loring, Caleb. By the Rev. Dr. Stillman, Mr. C. L., distiller, to the agreeable Miss Polly Selsbry. (S. May 5, 1792.)

* Died at Philadelphia, Mrs. Mary, amiable wife of Tobias Lear, Esq. (S. Aug. 10, 1793.)

Loring, John. Mr. J. L. to Miss Betsy Campbell, both of this town. (W. Feb. 27, 1788.)

Loring, Jonathan, jun. In this town, last evening, by the Rev. Mr. John Murray, Mr. J. L., jun., to Miss Nancy Haiden, both of Boston. (W. Nov. 27, 1793.)

Loring, Sally, m. William Bass.

Loring, Sally, m. Capt. Robran Drew.

Lothrop, Harriot, m. Chandler Robbins, jun.

Love, Jannet, m. James Thwing.

Lovedridge, Joseph. At Halifax, Mr. J. L. to Miss Mary Murphoy. (W. Nov. 7, 1792.)

Lovell, John M. J. M. L., Esq., to Mrs. Warner. (W. Aug. 11, 1790.)

Lovett, William. [At Beverly] Mr. W. L. to Miss Ruth Rea. (W. Feb. 27, 1793.)

Lovering, Joseph. Mr. J. L. to Mrs. Hannah Bowland. (W. Dec. 23, 1785.)

Low, S. At Weymouth, Mr. S. L., of Hingham, aged 76, to Mrs. Trask, aged 73. (S. Feb. 27, 1790.)

Low, Sally, m. Thomas Simmons.

Low, Samuel. Mr. S. L., of Lunenburg, to Miss Betsy Giddings, of Ipswich. (S. March 2, 1793.)

Ludlow, Gulian. At New York, Mr. G. L. to Miss Maria Ludlow.

Ludlow, Maria, m. Gulian Ludlow.

Lukeman, Dr. Nathan. At Salem, Dr. N. L., of Hamilton, to Miss Betsy Frye, of Salem. (W. Jan. 8, 1794.)

Lyle, James. At Philadelphia, Mr. J. L. to Miss Anne Hamilton, daughter of the late Andrew Hamilton, Esq. (S. Oct. 27, 1792.)

Lyman, Cornelius. [In this town] Capt. C. L., of the 2d United States Sub-Legion, to Miss Sally Mason, youngest daughter to Col. David Mason. (S. Jan. 26, 1793.)

Lyndes, Hannah, m. Edward Bangs.

Lyon, Rev. James. In this town, the Rev. J. L., of Machias, to Mrs. Skillings, widow of the late Mr. Samuel Skillings. (S. Nov. 30, 1793.)

Lyon, Lydia, m. Rufus Peck.

Lyon, Capt. John. At Rehoboth, Capt. J. L., of Leicester, to Miss Lydia Reed. (W. May 9, 1792.)

Lyon, Capt. John, jun., at Leicester, Capt. J. L., jun., to Mrs. Abigail Stickney. (W. Sept. 26, 1792.)

Lyon. See also Lion.

Lyons, Miss, m. John Hopkins.

Macallier, Lewis Lambert. [In this town] Mr. L. L. M. to Miss Lydia Fosdick, daughter of Mr. Alvin Fosdick, of this town. (S. July 19, 1794.)

M'Auly, John. At Poughkeepsie, Mr. J. M'A. to Miss Katy Sloan. (W. April 25, 1792.)

M'Call, Archibald, jun. At Philadelphia, Mr. A. M'C., jun., to Miss Elizabeth Cadwallader; and Mr. Samuel Ringgold to Miss Maria Cadwallader, both daughters of the late General Cadwallader. (S. May 19, 1792.)

M'Call, George. At Philadelphia, Mr. G. M'C., merchant, to Miss Margaret Clymer, eldest daughter of George Clymer, Esq., of that city. (S. May 31, 1794.)

M'Carthy, Elizabeth, m. Timothy Williams.

M'Clarey, Esther, m. Joseph Hartwell.

M'Clench, Samuel. In this town, Mr. S. M'C. to Miss Nancy Roberson. (W. Feb. 22, 1792.)

McClure, Sally, m. Capt. Edward Russell.

McClury, Polly, m. Silas Whitney.

Maccomber, Charles. At Westport, Mr. C. M. to the amiable Miss Peace Gifford, both of that place. (W. Sept. 25, 1793.)

M'Crea, William. At Baltimore, Mr. W. M'C. to Miss E. Thompson. (W. Feb. 29, 1792.)

M'Dougal, Mrs., m. Nathaniel Barret.

M'Evers, Eliza, m. John R. Livingston.

Mackay, Esther, m. Capt. John Page.

Mackay, Capt. John. At Salem, Capt. J. M., of this town, to the amiable Miss Boyd, of Portsmouth. (S. May 26, 1792.)

Mackay, Ruthy, m. Samuel W. Hunt.

Mackay, William, jun. In this town, Mr. W. M., jun., to Miss Amelia Hussey. (S. Nov. 3, 1792.)

M'Kinsey, John. On Sunday evening, Mr. J. M'K. to Miss Betsey Brown. (W. Oct. 6, 1790.)

M'Lane, Capt. [In Georgia] Capt. M'L. to Miss Hutchins, after a courtship of nine hours. (W. July 25, 1792.)

M'Lean, Anne, m. John Dodd.

M'Lellan, Eunice, m. Rev. Elijah Kellog.

McLintock, Rachel, m. John Creese.

McNeil, Hannah, m. Isaac Barrett.

Madey, J. J. At Olympia (Roxbury), by the Rev. Mr. Rousselet, M. J. J. M., of Martinique, to Madame de Cornet.* (W. Sept. 12, 1792.)

Madison, Hon. James. In Virginia, Hon. J. M., Esq., Member of Congress, to Mrs. Todd, of Philadelphia. (S. Oct. 18, 1794.)

Maenge, Catharine, m. François Duchemin.

Maglone, Hugh. At New-York, Mr. H. M. to Miss Polly White. (S. May 19, 1792.)

Makepeace, Sally, m. Jonathan Fowle.

Makepeace, Sukey, m. Ebenezer Larkin, jun.

Mallet, François. In this town, by the Rev. Dr. Stillman, Mr. F. M., of Normandy, in France, to Miss Sally Rogers, of Boston. (W. Dec. 25, 1793.)

Mallet, Michael. At Charlestown, Mr. M. M. to Miss Ruthy Adams. (S. Nov. 25, 1786.)

Mallett, Rachel, m. Ezra Welsh.

Malony, Michael. [In this town] Mr. M. M. to Miss Polly Inglesby. (S. Dec. 20, 1794.)

Mann, Aaron. Mr. A. M., of Providence, to Miss Grace S. Flagg, of this town. (S. June 6, 1789.)

Mann, Nancy, m. John Pray.

Mann, Newton. At Attleborough, Mr. N. M. to Miss Abigail Maxcy. (W. May 23, 1792.)

Manning, Howes. Mr. H. M. to Miss Polly Call, both of Charlestown. (S. May 24, 1788.)

Manning, William. At Bolton, Mr. W. M., printer, of this town, to Miss Lydia Brown, of that place. (S. May 24, 1794.)

Mansfield, Glover. Mr. G. M. to Miss Polly Akins. (W. Apr. 18, 1792.) At Danbury (Conn.) implied?

Mansfield, John. In this town, Mr. J. M. to Miss Sally Pritchard. (April 16, 1794.)

* After the nuptials were celebrated, the French ladies and gentlemen made a collection of above two hundred dollars, which were presented to the worthy and persecuted clergyman who performed the ceremony . . . , and who, as Catholick Missionary and Chaplin of the French families in Boston and its vicinity, has merited by his conduct the patronage he enjoys.

Mansfield, Joseph. In this town, Mr. J. M. to Miss Elizabeth Annis. (W. June 26, 1793.)

Mansfield, Sally, m. Capt. John Tucker.

Manwaring, Rebecca, m. Capt. Elisha Coit.

Marchant, Betsy, m. Thomas Sessions.

Marean, William. In this town, Mr. W. M. to Miss Sally Brewer, daughter of Col. David Brewer. (S. Sept. 21, 1793.)

Mark, Mr. [At Petersburg] Mr. M., of Prince George County, to Miss Patsy Lanier, of Petersburg. (W. July 11, 1792.)

Markol, Miss, m. Benjamin Franklin Bache.

Marks, Hannah, m. Capt. John Brewer.

Marlean, Sally, m. Samuel Colman.

Marryat, Joseph. J. M., Esq., of Grenada, to Miss Charlotte Geyer, daughter to Frederick William Geyer, Esq. (S. Dec. 19, 1789.)

Marsh, Deborah, m. Joseph Adams.

Marsh, Eunice, m. Darius Larned.

Marsh, Lydia, m. Joseph Sewall.

Marsh, Rhoda, m. Simon Poe.

Marshal, Betsy, m. Ezra Whitney.

Marshall, Betsey, m. John Baxter.

Marshall, Comfort, m. Benjamin Leverett.

Marshall, Polly, m. Edward Curtis.

Marshall, Thomas. [At Nantucket] Mr. T. M. to Miss Ruth Dow. (S. Dec. 15, 1792.)

Marson, Sarah, m. Ebenezer Tileston.

Marston, David. By the Rev. Mr. Elliot, Mr. D. M. to Miss Sally Tarr. (W. Nov. 22, 1786.)

> "At length he's come — come to dispel her fears,
> And rock the cradle of declining years."

Marston, Capt. Manassah. On Thursday evening last, the hymenial torch was light between Capt. M. M. and Miss Ingalls. When a refin'd sensibility is added to the most superlative worth, we cannot but presage that the alliance will do honour to the institution. (S. Jan. 29, 1785.)

Marston, Capt. Nathaniel. At Charleston (S.C.), Capt. N. M., of this town, to Miss Lydia Brown. (W. Sept. 8, 1790.)

Deaths, W. Dec. 26, 1792: At Charleston, S.C., Capt. Nathaniel Marston, late of the American Navy, and formerly of this town.

Marston, Mrs. Zerniah, m. Rev. Joseph Roby.

Martin, Katy, m. Thomas Hiller.

Martin, Knot, 3d. At Marblehead, Mr. K. M., 3d, to Miss Anna Abbot. (W. Oct. 1, 1794.)

Martin, Polly, m. Timothy Greene.

Martin, Susannah, m. William Boyd.

Martin, William. In South Carolina, Mr. W. M. to Miss B. Fenden. (S. March 3, 1792.)

Martyn, Sukey, m. Phineas Haskel, jun.

Mascoll, Hannah, m. Jesse Kenny.

Mason, Daniel. At Newton, Mr. D. M., of Lexington, to Mrs. Sally Cheney, of Newton. (S Feb. 9, 1793.)

Mason, Polly, m. Daniel Tuttle.

Mason, Sally, m. Cornelius Lyman.

Mason, Sukey, m. Rev. John Smith.

Masson, Mamy. In this town, Mr. M. M. to Miss Sally Farrington, eldest daughter of the late Capt. Joseph Farrington. (S. Dec. 28, 1793.)

Masury, see Musury.

Matchet, Capt. John. Capt. J. M., of this town, to Miss Elizabeth Perkins. (W. Jan. 4, 1786.)

Matlack, Miss, m. Joseph Stretch.

Matlack, Mary, m. Willet Hicks.

Matthews, Polly, m. John Mayo.

Matthewson, Rhoda, m. Benjamin Waterman.

Maxcy, Abigail, m. Newton Mann.

Maxcy, Rev. Jonathan. At Providence, Rev. J. M., Minister of the Baptist Church in that town, to Miss Susannah Hopkins. (W. Sept. 14, 1791.)

May, Lois, m. William Cunningham, jun.

May, Louisa, m. Benjamin Goddard.

May, Lucretia, m. Azor G. Archbald.

May, Maria, m. William Coolidge.

May, Nancy, m. Samuel Treet.

May, Patty, m. John Frothingham.

May, Perrin. In this town, Mr. P. M. to Miss Abigail Fellowes. (S. Nov. 14, 1789.)

May, Sally, m. Thomas Jackson.

Mayhew, Capt. Jeremiah. [At Martha's Vineyard] Capt. J. M., of New Bedford, to Mrs. Peggy Mayhew, of Chilmark. (S. Nov. 24, 1792.)

Mayhew, Jonathan. At Martha's Vineyard, Mr. J. M. to Miss Parnae Mayhew. (S. Nov. 24, 1792.)

Mayhew, Parnae, m. Jonathan Mayhew.

Mayhew, Mrs. Peggy, m. Capt. Jeremiah Mayhew.

Maynard, Samuel. In this town, by the Rev. Mr. Clarke, Mr. S. M., merchant, to Miss Deborah Coates, both of this town. (S. Dec. 31, 1791.)

Mayo, Ebenezer. [At Portland] Mr. E. M. to Miss Polly Foster Coffin. (W. July 18, 1792.)

Mayo, John. At Newton, Mr. J. M., of Roxbury, to Miss Polly Matthews. (S. Sept. 13, 1794.)

Mayo, Polly, m. William Cummenes.

Means, Peggy, m. Capt. John George.

Meeker, Phebe, m. Alexander Cochran.

Meeks, Edward. [At New York] Mr. E. M. to Miss Eliza Heyer. (S. Feb. 2, 1793.)

Meers, Russel. At Tewksbury, Mr. R. M. to the amiable Miss Susanna Duton. (S. Aug. 2, 1794.)

Megraw, Lucy, m. Samuel Flagg.

Mellen, Charlotte, m. William A. Kent.

Mercer, Nancy, m. Robert Patton.

Meriam, Anna, m. Edward Bodge.

Meriam, Sally, m. James Whipple, jun.

Merrick, Eunice, m. Maj. Ephraim Russell.

Merrick, Jonathan. At Newport (R.I.), Mr. J. M., of this town, to Miss Polly Peckham, of that city. (S. Jan. 21, 1786.)

Michaels, Peggy, m. Benjamin Sands.

Middleton, Nancy, m. Mr. Goddard.

Miercken, Miss, m. Richard Potter.

Miller, Betsy, m. Rev. James Coe.

Miller, Charles. In this town, C. M., Esq., to the amiable Miss Hannah Smith, daughter to the late Dr. Smith, of Newburyport. (W. Dec. 19, 1792.)

Miller, Joseph. At Cambridge, Mr. J. M., of Charlestown, to Miss Polly Tapley, of Cambridge. (W. Dec. 10, 1788.)

Millet, John. At Salem, Mr. J. M. to Miss Elizabeth Phillips. (W. Aug. 8, 1792.)
Milliquet, Peggy, m. Samuel Hughes, jun.
Mills, Ephraim. In this town, Mr. E. M., of Roxbury, to Miss Rebecca Gridley, of this place. (W. Nov. 13, 1793.)
Mills, Jane, m. David B. Mitchell.
Milne, Eliza, m. John Russell.
Minitree, Mary, m. N. Bowles.
Minns, Polly, m. Lemuel Tileston.
Minot, Hannah, m. J. H. Laugier, Baron de Taffy.
Mitchel, Jennet, m. Daniel Bryant.
Mitchell, David B. [In Savannah] D. B. M., Esq., to Miss Jane Mills. (S. March 3, 1792.)
Mitchell, Lucy, m. Joseph Hooper.
Mixter, Asa. At Shrewsbury, Mr. A. M. to the widow Ruth Murray, of Worcester. (S. Feb. 15, 1794.)
Moggin, Peggy, m. Benjamin Bolter.
Molineaux, Jenny, m. John Ripley.
Molly, John. At Hallowell, Mr. J. M. to Miss Patty Clark. (S. Feb. 9, 1793.)
Mongee, Samuel. At Baltimore, Mr. S. M., meadseller, Æt. 75, to Miss Spicer, mantua-maker, Æt. 18. (S. Nov. 23, 1793.)
Montmorency, Baron. In France, Baron M., aged 16, to a Lady, aged 14. (S. Sept. 20, 1788.)
Moody, Betsy, m. Daniel Philbrook.
Moody, Eliza, m. Joseph Ridgway, jun.
Moody, Esther Wheeler, m. Henry Sewall.
Moody, Jane, m. William Brabiner.
Moody, Nathaniel. At Portland, Mr. N. M. to Miss Jane Little. (W. Dec. 4, 1793.)
Moody, Polly, m. Thomas Bedlington.
Moody, Rebeckah, m. Capt. Joseph O'Brien.
Moody, Sarah, m. Amos Noyes.
Moore, Mrs., m. Capt. Amos Forward.
Moore, Hannah, m. Samuel Switcher.
Moore, Sally, m. Thomas Dawes Moore.
Moore, Thomas Dawes. Mr. T. D. M. to Miss Sally Moore, daughter of Mr. William Moore. (W. July 5, 1786.)

Moores, Eliza, m. Capt. David Folgier.

Moorhouse, Aaron. At Wilton, Mr. A. M. to Miss Parthena Gilbert. (W. July 4, 1792.)

More, Mary, m. William Greenough.

Morgan, Elias. At Hartford, Mr. E. M., merchant, to Miss Levina Bull. (S. Aug. 25, 1792.)

Morgan, Elias. At Hartford, Mr. E. M., merchant, to Mrs. Sally Smith. (W. Jan. 15, 1794.)

Morgan, William. In this town, Mr. W. M., of London (Eng.), to Miss Hannah Viburt, of this town. (S. May 24, 1794.) See also Viebart.

Morgan, William. In this town, Mr. W. M. to Miss Polly Weld. (W. Oct. 8, 1794.)

Morrill, Rev. Mr. At Salisbury (N.H.), Rev. Mr. Morrill, of Sedgwick (in Maine), to Miss Susannah Gale, of Salisbury. (S. Oct. 25, 1794.)

Morris, Mrs., m. Marmaduke Port.

Morris, Sally, m. Bethuel Gardner.

Morris, Sally, m. John Goldthwait.

Morris, Capt. Thomas. At Newburyport, Capt. T. M. to Miss Polly Rolf, both of that place. (W. Aug. 28, 1793.)

Morrison, Miss, m. Silas Cook.

Morrison, Michael. [At Newburyport] Mr. M. M. to Miss Paulina Chipman. (S. Nov. 1, 1794.)

Morse, Anna, m. William Eustis.

Morse, David. At Haverhill, Mr. D. M. to Miss Ruth Jo4nson. (W. June 11, 1794.)

Morse, Enoch. At Portland, Mr. E. M. to Miss Happy Thomas. (S. Feb. 4, 1792.)

Morse, Rev. Jedediah. In New-Jersey, Rev. J. M., of Charlestown, to Miss Breese. (W. June 3, 1789.)

Morse, Rev. John. At Medway, West Precinct, Rev. J. M., of Green-River (N.Y.), to Miss Clarissa Sanford; Rev. Ethan Smith, of Haverhill (N.H.), to Miss Bathsheba Sanford, eldest daughters to the Rev. Daniel Sanford. (S. March 2, 1793.)

Morse, Nabby, m. B. Allen, jun.

Morse, Robert. At Shaftsbury, Mr. R. M., 17 years of age, to Miss Charity Williams, in the 14th year of her age. (W. April 25, 1792.)

Morton, John. At Newport, Mr. J. M., of Philadelphia, to Miss Mary Robinson. (W. July 17, 1793.)

Morton, Peggy, m. Dr. Samuel Richardson.

Mosely, Samuel. At Dorchester, by the Rev. Mr. Harris, Mr. S. M., of Norwich (Conn.), to Miss Priscilla Baker, of Dorchester. (W. Jan. 1, 1794.)

Mossatt, Elizabeth Catherine, m. Nicholas Gysburtus Rousselet.

Moulder, Polly, m. William Duncan.

Moulton, Ebenezer. In this town, Mr. E. M. to Miss Nabby Bourne; Mr. N. W. Otis, of Charleston (S.C.), to Miss Nancy Bourne, daughters to the Hon. Shearjashub Bourne, Esq., M.C. (S. Nov. 1, 1694.)

Moultrie, Catharine, m. Dr. James Moultrie.

Moultrie, Dr. James. At Charleston (S.C.), Dr. J. M., son of the late Lieutenant-Governor of East Florida, to Miss Catharine Moultrie, daughter to Alexander Moultrie, Esq. (S. Dec. 11, 1790.)

Mountford, Mrs. Mary, m. James Treferen.

Mountfort, Mrs. Mary, m. Hon. Ebenezer Bridge.

Munroe, Oliver. At Shrewsbury, Mr. O. M., merchant, to Miss Lydia Flint, daughter of Dr. Edward Flint, of that town. (W. Feb. 12, 1794.)

Murphoy, Mary, m. Joseph Lovedridge.

Murray, James. At Charlestown, Mr. J. M. to Mrs. Rebecca Carr. (W. Aug. 22, 1792.)

Murray, John. At Salem, Mr. J. M., of Gloucester, Pastor of the Universal Society there, to Mrs. Judith Stevens, of that town. (W. Oct. 8, 1788.)

For an account of his installation at the "Universal Meeting House" in Boston, see S. Oct. 26, 1793.

Murray, Capt. Robert. At Halifax, Capt. R. M., of the British ship "l'Oiseau," to Miss Rebecca Halliburton, daughter of the Hon. John Halliburton. (S. Dec. 27, 1794.)

Murray, Ruth, m. Asa Mixter.

Musury, Samuel. At Salem, Mr. S. M. to Miss Nancy Brown. (S. Sept. 1, 1792.)

Myers, Samuel. At New York, Mr. S. M., merchant, of Petersburg (Va.), to Miss Sally Judal, of New-York. (W. Nov. 5, 1794.)

Myric, Love, m. Horatio Nichols.

Nancréde, P. J. G. de. By the Rev. Mr. Pancer, Mr. P. J. G. de N. to Miss Hannah Dixcey. (W. Nov. 12, 1788.)

Paul Joseph Guérard de Nancréde, instructor in French at Harvard, 1787–1800. In the Mass. Centinel, S. Jan. 3, 1789, he announced that he proposed to publish a weekly paper in French with the title "Courier de Boston."

Nash, Huldah, m. Pardon Potter.

Nash, Joshua. [In this town] Mr. J. N. to Miss Mary Stone. (S. May 12, 1792.)

Nash, Richard. Married at the Chapel church in this town, by the Rev. Mr. Parker, Mr. R. N., of Cornwall, in Great-Britain, to Miss Lucy Ann Apthorp, daughter of James Apthorp, Esq., of Braintree. (W. Sept. 28, 1785.)

Neale, Isaac. At Philadelphia, Mr. I. N., printer, to Miss Kammerer. (S. April 7, 1792.)

Neatt, Samuel. [In this town] Mr. S. N. to Miss Hannah Cushing. (W. Oct. 31, 1792.)

Nevers, Polly, m. William Wesson.

Newell, Eliphalet. Last Sunday evening, at Charlestown, by the Rev. Mr. Payne, E. N., Esq., to the amiable and engaging Miss Susannah Bradish, both of that town. (W. Aug. 15, 1787.)

Newell, Elizabeth, m. Cazneau Bayley.

Newell, Martha, m. Capt. Benjamin Homans.

Newell, Mary, m. Ebenezer Coffin.

Newell, Nabby, m. Thomas Badger.

Newell, Prudence, m. Isaac Smith, jun.

Newell, Sally, m. Joseph Brown.

Newson, Capt. John. In this town, by the Rev. Dr. Stillman, Capt. J. N., of Weathersfield (Conn.), to Mrs. Sally Tracy, of this town. (S. March 15, 1794.)

Neyle, Harriet, m. John Sollee.

Nice, Jacob. [At Philadelphia] Mr. J. N. to Miss Polly Berrett. (W. Feb. 13, 1793.)

Nichols, Eliza, m. Doctor Richard Perkins, jun.

Nichols, Horatio. At Nantucket, Mr. H. N., of Providence, to Miss Love Myric. (W. Oct. 23, 1793.)

Nichols, Sally, m. Benjamin Hammond.

Nicholson, Miss, m. Hon. Mr. Few.

Nicholson, Miss, m. Hon. Albert Gallaten.

Nicholson, Fanny, m. Hon. Joshua Sevey.
Nicholson, Henrietta, m. Dr. John Bracco.
Nicholson, Capt. Thomas. At Plymouth, Capt. T. N. to Miss Hannah Otis. (W. Feb. 4, 1789.)
Nickals, Katy, m. William Callender.
Nickels, Captain Alexander. [In this town] Captain A. N. to Miss Susannah Rust. (W. Dec. 3, 1794.)
Nickels, Polly, m. John Crocker Snow.
Nickles, William. At Philadelphia, Mr. W. N. to Miss Hilegas. (W. Feb. 13, 1793.)
Nightingale, Lydia, m. Abijah Warren.
Nisbett, Johanna, m. Capt. F. Garforth.
Nixon, Miss, m. Francis West.
Noble, Comfort, m. John Libbey.
Norcross, Mrs. Jenny, m. Thomas Whitman.
Norris, Patty, m. Enoch Churchman.
Norris, Ruth, m. Nathaniel Kingsbury.
North, Capt. Benjamin. At New-York, Capt. B. N. to Miss Sally Wicks, both of that city. (S. March 31, 1792.)
North, Major William. At New-York, Major W. N. to Miss Polly Duane, eldest daughter of James Duane [*sic*], Esq., Mayor of this city. (W. Oct. 24, 1787.)

Appleton's Cyc. of Amer. Biog. says: "Mary, daughter of Judge James Duane."

Northup, Mrs., m. Capt. John Carr.
Norton, Birdsey. At Goshen, Mr. B. N., merchant, to Miss Hannah Star. (S. Oct. 13, 1792.)
Norton, Rev. Jacob. At Braintree, Rev. J. N., of Weymouth, to Miss Betsy Cranch, eldest daughter to the Hon. Richard Cranch, Esq. (S. Feb. 21, 1789.)
Norton, Sally, m. Samuel Brewer.
Norton, Sally, m. Rev. John Elliot.
Norton, Capt. Thomas. Capt. T. N. to Miss Lydia Hammatt, of this town. (S. June 11, 1785.)

"When worth leads virtue to the hymenial shrine,
And love and friendship join the train — elate,
Cœlestial joys, and happiness divine,
Forever must attend the marriage state."

Norwood, Aby, m. William Barnett.
Nourse, Betsey, m. Uzziel Ray.
Nowell, Sally, m. Joseph Brown.

Noyes, Amos. [At Newbury-Port] Mr. A. N. to Miss Sarah Moody. (W. Jan. 15, 1794.)

Noyes, Dr. Nathaniel. In this town, Dr. N. N. to Miss Rebecca Hunt. (S. Sept. 3, 1791.)

Noyes, Mrs. Rebecca, m. Capt. Daniel Farley.

Noyes, Silas. Mr. S. N., of Newbury-Port, to Miss Dorcas Bradford, of this town. (S. Feb. 6, 1790.)

Nutty, Betty, m. B. Twentyman.

Nye, Sukey, m. Nathaniel Freeman.

Nye, Sukey, m. Ezra Smith.

O'Brien, Charles. Mr. C. O'B., mer., to Miss Patty Coskery. (W. Feb. 29, 1792.)

At Baltimore implied.

O'Brien, Capt. Joseph. At Newbury-Port, Capt. J. O'B., to Miss Rebeckah Moody, both of that town. (S. Nov. 18, 1786.)

Odiorne, George. At Exeter, Mr. G. O., of that place, to Miss Polly Bracket, of Quincy. (W. Dec. 24, 1794.)

Odiorne, Joanna, m. Rev. Jonathan Strong.

Ogden, Catharine, m. Abijah Hammond.

Oldfield, Eliza, m. William Eaton.

Oles, Nancy, m. Cornelius Lane.

Oliver, Betsy, m. Charles Pierce.

Oliver, Daniel. Mr. D. O., merchant, to Miss Abigail Thompson. (W. Nov. 7, 1787.)

Oliver, Elizabeth, m. Dr. Benjamin Waterhouse.

Oliver, Robert. [At Portsmouth] Mr. R. O. to Miss Mary Rand. (S. Nov. 22, 1794.)

Olney, Anstis, m. Thomas Rogerson.

Olney, Sally, m. James Gardner.

Orne, Hon. Azor. At Marblehead, the Hon. A. O., Esq., to the relict of the late Joshua Orne, Esquire. (W. May 10, 1786.)

Orne, Nancy, m. Samuel Gray.

Orphin, John B. At Nantucket, Mr. J. B. O. to Miss Susannah Gardner. (W. Sept. 14, 1793.)

Orr, Peggy, m. Miles Barnes.

Orton, James. At Pittsfield, Mr. J. O. to Miss Electra Graves. (S. May 26, 1792.)

Osborn, Gubbins. [At Salem] Mr. G. O. to Miss Nancy Cousins. (W. Apr. 17, 1793.)

Osborn, Lydia, m. William Bordman.

Osborne, Mrs., m. Major Cookson.

Osborne, Francis. At Petersburg, Mr. F. O. to Miss Nancy Turndull [Turnbull?]. W. July 11, 1792.)

Osborne, John, Mr. J. O., to the agreeable Miss Catherine Macaulay Barber, third daughter of Nat. Barber, Esq., deceased. (W. Mch. 28, 1792.)

Osgood, Isaac. At Salem, Isaac Osgood, Esq., to Miss Sally Pickman, daughter of the late Mr. Clarke Gayton Pickman. (W. Oct. 20, 1790.)

Appeared: To the memory of Mrs. Sally Osgood, the amiable consort of Isaac Osgood, Esq., who died at Salem, August, 1791, aged 20. (S. Aug. 20, 1791.)

Osgood, Polly, m. Paul Little, jun.

Osut, Miss, m. Mr. Liillielbridge.

Otis, Dr. Galen. Dr. G. O., of Bromfield, to Miss Joanna Tilden, daughter of Major David Tilden, of this town. (S. Nov. 26, 1785.)

Otis, Hannah, m. Capt. Thomas Nicholson.

Otis, Harrison Gray. By the Rev. Mr. Parker, H. G. O., Esq., to Miss Sally Foster, daughter of William Foster, Esq. (S. June 5, 1790.)

Otis, N. W. [In this town] Mr. N. W. O., of Charleston, (S. C.) to Mrs. Nancy Bourne. (Nov. 1, 1794.)

See also Ebenezer Moulton.

Outram, Miss, m. Capt. Edward Davis.

Packard, Rev. Asa. At Braintree, the Rev. Asa Packard, of Marlborough, to Miss Nancy Quincy, youngest daughter of the late Col. Josiah Quincy. (S. July 31, 1790.)

Page, Capt. Benjamin. At Providence, Capt. B. P. to Miss Ann Sweeting. (S. Nov. 19, 1791.)

Page, Capt. John. At Salem, Capt. J. P. to Miss Esther Mackay, daughter of Capt. Daniel Mackay. (W. Feb. 1, 1792.)

Page, Polly, m. Nathaniel Copeland.

Paine, Amasa. At Westminster (Vermont), A. P., Esq., Attorney-at-law, to Miss Betsey Hower, daughter of the late Capt. Benjamin Hower, of this town. (W. Sept. 29, 1787.)

Paine, Nathaniel. At Worcester, Mr. N. P., Attorney-at-law, to the amiable Miss Elizabeth Chandler, second daughter of the late Gardner Chandler, Esq., of that town, deceased. (W. Dec. 28, 1785.)

Paine, Sally, m. James Perkins.

Paine, William. At Parsonsfield, Mr. W. P. to Miss Hannah Kinsman. (W. Jan. 8, 1794.)

Paleske, Charles Godfried. At Philadelphia, C. G. P., Esq., his Prussian Majesty's Counsel General to the United States of America, to Miss Hannah Elmslie, of that city. (S. May 12, 1792.)

Palfrey, Hannah, m. Jonathan Trask.

Palfrey, Susan, m. William Lee, jun.

Palfrey, Mrs. Susannah, m. Constant Freeman.

Palmer, Eden. [At Danbury] Mr. E. P. to Miss Betsey Bartram. (S. Apr. 7, 1792.)

Palmer, Hannah, m. Richard Yates.

Parker, Elias. On Wednesday evening, by the Rev. Dr. Parker, E. P., Esq., Captain in the late American Army, to the amiable Mrs. Mary Brown of this place. (S. Oct. 2, 1790.)

Parker, Rev. Frederick. At Canterbury, Rev. F. P. to Miss Sukey Foster. (S. Dec. 7, 1793.)

Parker, Isaac. In this town, I. P., Esq., of Penobscot, to Miss Rebecca Hall, of this town. (W. June 25, 1794.)

Parker, Jemima, m. John Pigeon.

Parker, Katy, m. Ebenezer Brown.

Parker, Mrs. Meriam, m. Charles Coffin.

Parker, Nathaniel. At Exeter, N. P., Esq., to Miss Catharine Tilton. (W. Dec. 4, 1793.)

Parker, Polly, m. Loring Bailey.

Parker, Rebecca, m. Samuel Vickary.

Parker, Samuel L. In this town, Mr. S. L. P. to Miss Ruth Adams, daughter to the late Capt. John Adams. (S. Oct. 1, 1791.)

Parkman, William. At Concord, at the house of Duncan Ingraham, Esq., Mr. W. P. to the amiable Miss Lydia Proctor. (S. Jan. 31, 1789.)

Parks, Warham. At Charleston, W. P., Esq., of Westfield, to Miss Gorham, eldest daughter of Nathaniel Gorham, Esq. (S. Dec. 24, 1791.)

Parrot, Elizabeth, m. Jean Toscan.

Parry, Edward. At Portsmouth, m. E. P., mer., to Miss Johanna Chauncey. (S. Nov. 15, 1794.)

Parsons, Elizabeth W., m. Amos Rhodes.

Parsons, Mrs. Martha, m. Edward Rand.

Passmore, Thomas. At Portsmouth, Mr. T. P., of Philadelphia, to Miss Eliza Pierce. (W. May 21, 1794.)

Passmore, Thomas. Mr. T. P. to Miss Eliza Peirce. (S. May 31, 1794.)

Patchan, Ralph. At New York, Mr. R. P., to Miss Fanny Yorkison. (S. June 23, 1792.)

Patrick, Isabella, m. John Spooner.

Patson [Payson?], Samuel. At Dorchester, Mr. S. P. to Miss Sally Trescot. (W. Apr. 13, 1791.)

Patten, Nathaniel. At Long-Meadow, Mr. N. P., mer., of Hartford, to Miss Sally Burt. (W. Mch. 7, 1792.)

Patten, Nathaniel. In this town, Mr. N. P. to Miss. Nancy Scott. (W. Oct. 31, 1792.)

Patten, Polly, m. Thomas Hunt.

Patten, Robert. At Fredericksburg (Virginia), Mr. R. P., merchant, to Miss Nancy Mercer, daughter to the late Gen. Hugh Mercer. (W. Nov. 14, 1792.)

Paulding, Julia, m. William Irving, jun.

Payne, Sally, m. Dr. Miles Littlejohn.

Payson, Henry. In this town, H. P., Esq., of Baltimore, merchant, to Miss Eunice Crosby, of this town. (S. Apr. 6, 1793.)

Payson, Phillips, jun. At Charlestown, on Tuesday evening last, P. P., jun., Esq., to Miss Ruthy Larkin, eldest daughter of Deacon John Larkin, of that town. (S. Apr. 6, 1793.)

Payson, Samuel. In this town, Mr. S. P., of Charlestown, to Miss Grace Welsh. (S. Dec. 18, 1790.)

Pearce, Capt. Robert. Capt. R. P., of Nova-Scotia, to Miss Polly Townsend. (S. Nov. 19, 1791.)
At Newport implied.

Pease, David. [At Nantucket] Mr. D. P., to Miss Sally Forsdick. (W. Sept. 14, 1793.)

Pebbles, Hugh. At Lansingburg, H. P., Esq., to Miss Abigail Serrat, of Newport, R.I. (S. Dec. 20, 1794.)

Peale, Abigail Mason, m. John Dabney.
Pearce, Bethiah, m. Robert Williams.
Pearce, Sally, m. John Williams.
Pease, Mrs., m. Thomas Crane.
Pease, Mercy, m. John Read.
Peck, Miss, m. Edwards Ely.
Peck, Nancy B., m. Edward Stow.
Peck, Mrs. May, m. Hon. Walter Spooner.
Peck, Rufus. At Woodstock, Mr. R. P. to Miss Lydia Lyon. (W. Feb. 13, 1793.)
Peckham, Polly, m. Jonathan Merrick.
Peete, Rebecca, m. Benjamin Seward.
Pelham, Helena, m. Thomas Curtis.
Peirce, Ann, m. John Lathrop, jun.
Peirce, Betsy, m. Reuben Blake.
Peirce, David. At Gloucester, D. P., Esq., to Miss Nabby Ingersol. (W. Dec. 19, 1792.)
Peirce, Eliza, m. Thomas Passmore.
Peirce, Mrs. Elizabeth, m. Capt. John Derby.
Peirce, Heman. Mr. H. P. to Miss Polly Bowen. (S. July 6, 1793.)
In this town implied.
Penhallow, Polly, m. Daniel Austin.
Penniman, Atherton. In this town, Mr. A. P. to Miss Abigail Butterfield. (W. June 11, 1794.)
Pepper, Capt. Isaac. In this town, Capt. I. P. to Miss Polly Harris Edes [both of this town]. (S. Dec. 15, 1792.)
Perket, John. In this town, Mr. J. P. to Miss Elizabeth Poole. (W. July 24, 1793.)
Perkins, Mrs. Abigail, m. Doct. Nathaniel S. Prentiss.
Perkins, Elizabeth, m. Hon. Stephen Higginson.
Perkins, Elizabeth, m. Capt. John Matchet.
Perkins, James. At Worcester, Mr. J. P., of this town, to Miss Sally Paine, daughter of the Hon. Timothy Paine, Esq., of that place. (W. Jan. 25, 1786.)
Perkins, James. Mr. J. P. to Mrs. Mary Donnells [both of this town]. (W. Nov. 17, 1790.)
Perkins, Nabby, m. Benjamin Weld.
Perkins, Doctor, Richard, jun., at Whitestown (N.Y.) Doctor R. P., jun., formerly of Bridgwater, in this State,

to the amiable Miss Eliza Nichols, of that place. (W. Dec. 21, 1791.)

Perkins, Sally, m. Hon. Stephen Higginson.

Perkins, Samuel. [In this town] Mr. S. P. to Miss Call. (S. May 18, 1793.)

Perkins, Thomas. Mr. T. P., merchant, to Miss Charlotte Appleton, daughter to Nathaniel Appleton, Esq. (W. Jan. 21, 1789.)

Perkins, Thomas H. Mr. T. H. P., merchant, to Miss Sally Elliot, only daughter of Mr. Simon Elliot. (W. Mch. 26, 1788.)

Perry, John. In this town, Mr. J. P. to Miss Catherine Grough. (S. Dec. 27, 1794.)

Peters, William B. In this town, Mr. W. B. P. to Miss Mary Purkett. (S. June 21, 1794.)

Pettis, Lydia, m. Capt. Matthew Hanly.

Phelon, Major Edward. At Charleston (S. C.) Major E. P., of the Massachusetts line of the late army, to Miss Susannah Frances Barksdale, of that city — a young lady of merit. (S. Feb. 21, 1789.)

Phelps, William. [At Salem] Mr. W. P., to Miss Sarah Punchard. (W. Jan. 2, 1793.)

Philbrook, Daniel. At Bath, Mr. D. P. to Miss Betsy Moody. (S. Feb. 9, 1893.)

Phille, Mary, m. John Knapp.

Phillips, Elizabeth, m. John Millet.

Phillips, Mrs. Christina, m. Capt. John Brown.

Phillips, Hannah, m. Samuel Shaw.

Phillips, Israel. At Greenfield, Mr. I. P. to Miss Mercy Bascom. (W. Nov. 26, 1794.)

Phillips, James. At Ipswich, Mr. J. P., of this town, to Miss Sally Farley, daughter to the late Hon. Michael Farley, Esq., of that place. (W. Dec. 19, 1792.)

Phillips, John. In this town, by the Rev. Dr. Howard, J. P., Esq., attorney-at-law, to Miss Sally Walley, both of this town. (S. Dec. 20, 1794.)

Phillips, Lucy, m. Ephraim Jones.

Phillips, Lydia, m. William Story, junr.

Phillips, Mary, m. Rev. Dr. Bass.

Phillips, Patty, m. Reuben Gould.

Phillips, Peggy, m. Samuel Cooper.

Phillips, Polly, m. Dr. William Spooner,

Phillips, Sally, m. Edward Dowse.

Phillips, Hon. William. In this town, on Thursday morning last, the Hon. W. P., Esq., to Mrs. Sarah Beck, both of this town. (S. June 23, 1792.)

Philips, Hannah, m. John Ireland.

Phipps, Samuel. In this town, Mr. S. P. to Miss Eliza Howard. (S. Nov. 29, 1794.)

Pick, Jacobus. On Sunday evening, Mons. J. P. to Miss Elizabeth Bradshaw, of the Boston Theatre. (S. July 12, 1794.)

Pickard, Polly, m. Benjamin Brown.

Pickering, Betsy, m. John Symonds.

Pickman, Sally, m. Isaac Osgood

Pico, Richard Lane. Mr. R. L. P. to Miss Hannah Gore, both of this town. (W. May 7, 1794.)

Pierce, Col. At New York, Col. P., Paymaster-General of the army, to Miss Nancy Bard, daughter of Dr. Bard, an eminent physician of that city. (S. Nov. 18, 1786.)

Pierce, Charles. In this town, Mr. C. P. to Miss Betsy Oliver. (W. Mch. 13, 1793.)

Pierce, Eliza, m. Thomas Passmore.

Pierce, Isaac. Mr. I. P. to Mrs. Joanna Harris, widow of the late Capt. Josiah Harris, formerly of Charlestown. (W. Mch. 14, 1787.)

Pierce, John. In this town, by the Rev. Dr. Stillman, Mr. J. P., to Mrs. Sally Lobdell, both of this town. (W. Jan. 4, 1792.)

Pierce, Sally, m. Isaac Edes.

Pierce, Samuel. Last week, by the Rev. Mr. Eliot, Mr. S. P. to Miss Hannah Luther Tyler. (S. Oct. 8, 1791.)

Pierce, Samuel. At Easton, Mr. S. P., of Dorchester, to Miss Polly Lathrop, of Easton. (S. May 12, 1792.)

Pierpont, Sally, m. William Taylor.

Pierson, Betsy, m. Samuel Boyd.

Pierson, Rachel, m. Richard Fox.

Pigeon, Henry. At Newton, Mr. H. P., merchant, to Miss Betsy Starr. (W. May 5, 1790.)

Pigeon, John. At Newton, Mr. J. P., merchant, to the agreeable Miss Jemima Parker, both of that town. (W. Feb. 10, 1790.)

Pillsbury, Elizabeth, m. Samuel Dennis.

Pilsbury, Thomas. At Leak (Eng.), Mr. T. P., aged 76, to Miss Mary Turnock, aged 21 [taking the fourth wife]. (W. Jan. 2, 1793.)

Pinckney, Brigadier-General. At Charleston (S.C.), the Hon. Brigadier-General Pinckney to Miss Stead. (W. Sept. 6, 1786.)

Pinkham, Susannah, m. Barker Turner.

Pitcher, John. Mr. J. P. to Miss Elizabeth Jordan, both of Andover. (S. Jan. 28, 1792.)

Pittengill, Mrs. Abigail, m. Samuel Smith.

Pixley, Mrs. Abigail, m. James Root.

Plater, Miss, m Hon. Uriah Forrest.

Platt, Elizabeth, m. David S. Bogart.

Platt, Jennet, m. Abel Foot.

Platt, Col. Richard. At New York, Col. Richard Platt to Miss Sally Aspinwall, of Flushing. (S. Sept. 25, 1790.)

Plumer, Sally, m. Thomas Smith.

Poe, Simon. In North Carolina, Mr. S. P., aged 84, to Miss Rhoda Marsh, aged 58: The bridegroom has now living 186 children, grandchildren, and great-grandchildren. (W. Oct. 3, 1792.)

Polley, Simeon. In this town Mr. S. P. to the agreeable Miss Sally Ridgeway Stutson. (S. Jan. 12, 1788.)

Pomeroy, Major Samuel W. At Middletown, Major S. W. P., of Cambridge, in this state, to Miss Clarissa Alsop, of Middleton. (S. Sept. 21, 1793.)

Pond, Prudence, m. Daniel Gealy.

Pool, Ebenezer. At Hull, Mr. E. P. to Miss Sarah Gould. (W. Oct. 1, 1794.)

Poole, Elizabeth, m. John Perket.

Poole, Mary, m. Capt. Jonathan Ingersoll.

Poole, Nancy, m. Yachel Dorsey.

Poor, Catharine, m. William Cook.

Pope, Edward, E.P., of Bedford, Esq., to Mrs. Elizabeth Elliot, widow of the late Mr. Samuel Elliot, and daughter of William Greenleaf, Esq., of this town. (S. June 11, 1785.)

Pope, Hannah, m. Joseph Balch, Jun.

Pope, Joshua. [At Salem] At the Friend's Meeting-House, Mr. J. P. to Miss Bethiah Dean. (S. Sep. 3, 1791.)

Port, Marmaduke. [At Philadelphia] Mr. M. P. to Mrs. Morris, the former 83, the latter 67 years of age. (W. Feb. 13, 1793.)

Porter, Betsey, m. Nathaniel Gould.

Porter, Capt. Charles. By the Rev. Mr. Belknap, Capt. C. P. to Miss Betsy Wilkinson. (W. Oct. 5, 1791.)

Porter, Lucy, m. Ebenezer Blin.

Porter, Ruth, m. Moses Stone.

Porter, Thomas. At Alexandria (Virginia), Mr. T. P., formerly of this State, to Miss Sally Ramsay. (W. March 5, 1788.)

Potter, Anthony. At Concord (N.H.), Mr. A. P. to Miss Dolly Goodwin, of Warner. (S. Nov. 2, 1793.)

Potter, Pardon. At New Bedford, Mr. P. P. to Miss Huldah Nash. (S. Nov. 23, 1793.)

Potter, Polly, m. Gamaliel Bryant, Jun.

Potter, Richard. At Philadelphia, R. P. merchant, to Miss Miercken. (S. Dec. 11, 1790.)

Potter, Sally, m. William Haskins.

Potts, Anna, m. Edward Key.

Powel, Benjamin. At Springfield, Mr. B. P. to Miss Polly Dwight, of Long Meadow. From the first of January last to the 18th of July inst. Mr. Powell has travelled in the publick stages seven thousand three hundred and sixty miles. (W. July 23, 1788.)

Powell, Snelling. In this town, last evening, at the Rev. Mr. Murray's Universal Meeting-house, Mr. S. P. to Miss Betsy Harrison, both of the company of comedians in this town. (W. July 9, 1794.)

A critic, under the name "Spectator," had written on March 8: "Mr. S. Powell will ever please, particularly when he shines under the influence of Miss Harrison, and we must always regret the separation of a pair so congenial, so formed to throw additional lustre upon the accomplishments of each other." Mr. Powell and the critic seem to have been of one mind. The same writer says: "Miss Harrison beggars description: beauty, elegance, sensibility, and genius are her attributes. In adapting, in dressing, in *looking* the CHARACTER, she is a prodigy in whom our wishes are equalled and our expectations excelled."

Powell, William. W. P., Esq., to Mrs. Gardner. (S. Apr. 4, 1789.)

Pratt, Mrs. Abigail, m. Ziba Crane.

Pratt, Rev. Allen. At Marshfield, by the Rev. Elijah Leonard, the Rev. A. P., of Westmorland, to Miss Persis Little, of Marshfield. (W. Feb. 8, 1792.)

Pratt, Cloe, m. Major Jeremiah Conant.

Pratt, Olive, m. John Fenno.

Pratt, William. At Salem, Mr. W. P., to Miss Mary Williams. (W. Nov. 21, 1792.)

Pray, Miss, m. Silas Ballou.

Pray, John. At Great Ogechee, Mr. J. P. to Miss Nancy Mann. (S. Sept. 8, 1792.)

Pray, John. [At New York] Mr. J. P. to Miss Sally Crone [Crane?] (S. Feb. 2, 1793.)

Preble, Samuel. At Salem, Mr. S. P., merchant, to Miss Polly Derby. (W. June 15, 1785.)

Preble, Statira, m. Capt. Richard Codman.

Precec, Marquiss. At New York, the marquiss P. to Miss Livingston, of Rhinebec. (S. Oct. 19, 1793.)

Premir, Mrs. Polly, m. John Jutau.

Prentiss, Rev. Mr. The Rev. Mr. Prentiss, of Medfield, to Miss Mary Scollay, daughter of John Scollay, Esq., of this town. (S. Feb. 14, 1789.)

Prentiss, Appleton. Last evening, Mr. A. P., merchant, to Miss Silence Conant, a young lady in whom is indeed every amiable qualification. (W. June 15, 1785.)

Prentiss, Margaret, m. Rev. Timothy Dickerson.

Prentiss, Margaret, m. Nehemiah Rand.

Prentiss, Doct. Nathaniel S., at Marlboro', Doct. N. S. P. to Mrs. Abigail Perkins. (S. Nov. 24, 1792.)

Prentiss, Sally, m. John A. Laurence.

Prescot, Miss, m. Timothy Bigelow.

Prescott, James, Jun. At New-Ipswich, Newhampshire, J. P., Jun., Esq., of Westford, Massachusetts, to the agreeable Miss Hannah Champney, daughter of the Hon. Ebenezer Champney, Esq., of that place. (S. Feb. 18, 1792.)

Prescott, William. At Salem, W. P., Esq., of that town, to Miss Catharine Hicklin. (S. Dec. 28, 1793.)
Mar. Dec. 18. Parents of William Hickling Prescott.

Preston, Becca, m. John Hubbard.

Preston, Remember, Jun. In this town, Mr. R. P., Jun., to Miss Sally Clark. (W. Dec. 4, 1793.)

Price, Polly, m. Thomas Greenleaf.

Prince, Capt. James. At Charlestown, Capt. J. P., of this town, to Miss Agnes Gordon, of that place. (W. Feb. 25, 1789.)

Prince, Maria, m. John Beckley.

Prince, Mary, m. Charles Apthrop.

Prince, Sally Henshaw, m. John Tucker.

Prince, Samuel. Last Sunday evening, Mr. S. P. to Miss Sarah Ingersol. (W. Oct. 18, 1786.)

Prince, Capt. Samuel. In this town, Capt. S. P. to Miss Frances Davis. (W. May 22, 1793.)

Prior, Joshua. Mr. J. P. to Miss Betsey Fellows. (S. April 14, 1792.)
At Lebanon implied.

Prisely, Polly, m. Robert Robertson, Jun.

Procter, William. At Lynn, Mr. W. P. to Mrs. Anna Brown. (S. Jan. 19, 1793.)

Procter, William B. In this town, Mr. W. B. P. to Miss Lydia Bowes. (S. Jan. 26, 1793.)

Proctor, Miss, m. William Shaw.

Proctor, Col. Edward. In this town, Col. E. P. to Miss Polly Adams. (W. Aug. 25, 1790.)

Proctor, Col. Edward. Col. E. P. to Miss Hannah Atkins. (W. June 22, 1791.)

Proctor, Lydia, m. William Parkman.

Proctor, Thorndike, Jun. At Salem, Mr. T. P., Jun., to Betsey Hathorne. (W. Apr. 9. 1788.)

Prout, Lydia, m. Samuel Cutler.

Province, Eliza, m. Samuel Dexter.

Puffer, James. At Shrewsbury, Mr. J. P., of Sudbury, to Mrs. Submit Goddard, of Shrewsbury. (W. March 14, 1792.)

Punchard, Sarah, m. William Phelps.

Purkett, Mary, m. William B. Peters.

Putnam, Dr. Archelaus. At Danvers, by the Rev. Mr. Osgood, Dr. A. P. to Miss Nabby Bishop, both of said town. (W. Nov. 15, 1786.)

Putnam, Ebenezer. At Salem, Mr. E. P. to Miss Sally Fisk, daughter of Brigadier-General Fisk. (W. May 25, 1791.)

Putnam, Eliza, m. Winthrop Gray.

Putnam, Sally, m. Dr. Nahum Fay.

Quackembos, Nancy, m. Thomas Greenleaf.

Quincey, John W. In this town, last Thursday evening, Mr. J. W. Q., of Portland, merchant, to Miss Abigail Atkins, daughter of Capt. Silas Atkins, of this town. (W. May 7, 1794.)

Quincey, Samuel. Mr. S. Q., attorney-at-law, to Miss Elizabeth Hatch, daughter of Col. Jabez Hatch, both of this town. (W. Nov. 1, 1786.)

Quincy, Edmund. Last Thursday evening, by the Rev. Mr. Thatcher, the Hon. E. Q., Esq., to Miss Anna Gerrish, a maiden lady of agreeable and engaging manners. (W. Jan. 18, 1785.)

Quincy, Nancy, m. Rev. Asa Packard.

Quincy, Polly, m. James Kettle.

Quynn, Miss, m. Capt. John Kilty.

Ramsay, Sally, m. Thomas Porter.

Ramsdell, Betsey, m. Levi Starbuck.

Rand, Edward. At Newburport, Mr. E. R., merchant, to Mrs. Martha Parsons. (S. Oct. 27, 1792.)

Rand, Joanna, m. Caleb Lamson.

Rand, Mary, m. Robert Oliver.

Rand, Nehemiah. At Cambridge, on Monday last, N. R., Esq., of Lindsborough, to Miss Margaret Prentiss, daughter of the late Rev. Thomas Prentiss, of Charlestown. (W. Nov. 23, 1791.)

Rand, Thomas. At Charlestown, Mr. T. R. to Miss Polly Larkin. (S. Jan. 18, 1894.)

Ranger, Fanny, m. Jedidiah Joy.

Rathbon, Joshua. At Providence, Mr. J. R. to Miss Wait Kilton. (W. Oct. 8, 1794.)

Ray, Uzziel. At Salem, Mr. U. R. to Miss Betsey Nourse. (S. Nov. 20, 1790.)

Raymond, Benjamin. At Nantucket, Mr. B. R. to Miss Betsey Kidder. (S. Dec. 14, 1793.)

Raymond, Ephraim. At Raynham, Mr. E. R., formerly of this town, to Miss Polly Dean, daughter of Josiah Dean, Esq., of that place. (S. Nov. 8, 1788.)

Rea, Betsey, m. Capt. Michael Homer.

Rea, Betsey, m. Capt. Zechariah Rhodes.

Rea, Daniel, tertius. Mr. D. R., tertius, to Miss Sally Bangs. (W. April 22, 1789.)

Rea, Ruth, m. William Lovett.

Rea, William. At Murphy'sboro' (N.C.), Mr. W. R., merchant, formerly of Boston, to Miss Peggy Wynn, of Salem. (S. Feb. 16, 1793.)

Read, Mrs. Harriott, m. James Crosby.

Read, Gen. James. At Leominster, Gen. J. R. to Miss Mary Farrar. (S. March 16, 1793.)

Read, John. In this town, Mr. J. R. to Miss Mercy Pease. (W. Feb. 18, 1789.)

Read, Thomas. On Thursday, Mr. T. R. to the amiable Miss Ruthy Wait, both of Roxbury. (W. March 12, 1788.)

Redman, Patty, m. Joseph A. Kimble.

Reed, Amos. Near Poughkeepsie, Mr. A. R. to Mrs. Roby Jinks. (S. May 7, 1791.)

The story which follows was printed again S. March 31, 1792, where the bride's name, *Miss* Roby Jenks, gives the narrative an entirely different aspect.

Reed, Joshua. By the Rev. Mr. Holmes, Mr. J. R. to Miss Susannah Boardman, both of Cambridge. (S. March 1, 1794.)

Reed, Lydia, m. Capt. John Lyon.

Reed, Dr. William. [In this town] by the Rev. Dr. Walter, Dr. W. R. to Miss Eliza Hall, daughter to Mr. Stephen Hall, of this town. (W. Jan. 9, 1793.)

Rees, James. [At Philadelphia] Mr. J. R. to Miss Eliza Reynolds. (S. Nov. 17, 1792.)

Reinecker, Clarinda, m. Cornelius Howard Gist.

Relse, Nancy, m. Henry Doggett.

Remington, Rev. Jesse. At Deerfield, Rev. J. R. of Condia, to Miss Polly Jennes. (W. Dec. 4, 1793.)

Revere, Fanny, m. Thomas Eayres.

Rexford, Jordan. At Marblehead, Mr. J. R., an *itinerent Methodist preacher*, of Connecticut, to Mrs. Sarah Barker, of that town. (W. May 7, 1794.)

Reynolds, Edward. Mr. E. R. to Miss Debby Belcher. (S. June 26, 1790.)

Reynolds, Eliza, m. James Rees.

Reynolds, George. At Salem, Mr. G. R. to Miss Nabby Ervin. (W. Jan. 2, 1793.)

Reynolds, Patty, m. Rev. Mr. Barcom.

Reynolds, Polly, m. Rev. Mr. Kinsbury.

Rhea, Sally, m. Nathaniel Cabot Higginson.

Rhodes, Amos. At Lynn, Mr. A. R., merchant, to Miss Elizabeth W. Parsons. (S. June 28, 1794.)

Rhodes, Capt. Zechariah. Capt. Z. R. to Miss Betsey Rea. (S. March 26, 1785.)

Rice, John. Mr. J. R., aged 19, to Miss Elizabeth Wheelock, aged 21. (W. Dec. 1, 1790.)

Rice, John. Mr. J. R., a bachelor, near 70 years of age, of a respectable character and fortune, to a young lady of 19, both of Charlotte county, Virginia. (W. Dec. 5, 1792.)

Rice, Dr. Samuel. At Worcester, Dr. S. R. to Miss Nancy Woodburn. (S. Sept. 21, 1793.)

Rich, Lydia, m. Charles Clements.

Richards, Ebenezer. At Newton, Mr. E. R. to Miss Hannah White. (S. May 4, 1793.)

Richards, George. Mr. G. R. to the amiable Mrs. Sally Wallace. (S. Apr. 22, 1786.)

Richards, Susanna, m. Josiah Edson.

Richardson, Abigail, m. Thomas Rumrill.

Richardson, Nathaniel H. Mr. N. H. R. to Miss Mary Dwight Coverly, . . . of this town. (S. Oct. 5, 1793.)

Richardson, Richard. Mr. R. R. to Miss Martha Harding, daughter to the late Capt. Thomas Harding, of Charlestown. (W. June 16, 1790.)

Richardson, Dr. Samuel. At Colrain, Dr. S. R., of Whittingham, to Miss Peggy Morton, of this town. (W. May 23, 1792.)

Ridgaway, Sukey, m. Peter Gade.

Ridgway, James. Mr. J. R., of this town, to Mrs. Catharine Stimpson, of Reading. (S. Feb. 5, 1797.)

Ridgway, James. In this town, Mr. J. R. to Miss Susannah Sumner. (S. Nov. 9, 1793.)

Ridgway, Joseph, Jun. At Newbury, New-Town, Mr. J. R., Jun., to Miss Eliza Moody. (S. Dec. 27, 1794.)

Ridgway, Mary, m. Jonathan Wild.

Ridgway, Samuel. In this town, Mr. S. R. to Mrs. Sarah Greaton, widow of the late Gen. Greaton. (W. Feb. 6, 1793.)

Riggs, Massy, m. Thomas Wheeler.

Riley, James. At Baltimore, Mr. J. R. to Miss Ann Lee. (W. April 25, 1792.)

Rindge, Olive, m. Col. Nathaniel Folsom.

Ringgold, Samuel. [At Philadelphia] Mr. S. R. to Miss Maria Cadwallader. (S. May 19, 1792.)

See, also, Archibald M'Call.

Ripley, John. Mr. J. R. to Miss Jenny Molineaux [both of this town.] (S. Aug. 6, 1791.)

Ripley, Capt. Joseph. Capt. J. R., of Kingston, to Miss Elizabeth Wallis, daughter of Mr. Samuel Wallis, merchant. (S. June 22, 1793.)

In this town implied.

Rittenhouse, John. [In this town] Mr. J. R. to Miss Polly Whitten. (S. April 5, 1794.)

Roach, John. At New York, Mr. J. R., of St. Croix, to Miss Sarah T. Halstead, of that city. (W. Sept. 3, 1794.)

Roach, Nancy, m. Joseph Waldren.

Robbins, Chandler, Jun. At Plymouth, Mr. C. R., Jun., of Hallowell, to Miss Harriot Lothrop. (W. Sept. 18, 1793.)

Robbins, Hannah, m. Benjamin Gilman.

Robbins, Nancy, m. Jacob Thompson.

Robbins, Sukey, m. John Clapp.

Robbins, Susannah, m. Phineas Woodman.

Roberdeau, Capt. At Newbury Port, Capt. R. to Miss Sarrah Tappan, of that place. (W. Aug. 16, 1786.)

Roberson, Nancy, m. Samuel M'Clench.

Roberts, Polly, m. Capt. John Gray.

Robertson, Betsey, m. Samuel Robertson.

Robertson, Joseph. In this town, by the Rev. Docter Stillman, Mr. J. R. to Miss Jenny Beals. (W. Dec. 28, 1791.)

Robertson, Robert, Jun. Mr. R. R., Jun., to Miss Polly Prisely [both of this town.] (S. Oct. 23, 1790.)

Robertson, Samuel. Mr. S. R. to Miss Betsey Robertson, [both of this town.] (S. Oct. 23, 1790.)

Robins, Jonathan D. In this town, by Rev. Mr. Kirkland, Mr. J. D. R. to Miss Fanny Crafts, daughter to Thomas Crafts, Esq. (S. Dec. 13, 1794.)

Robinson, Miss, m. Dr. Holbrook.

Robinson, Almy, m. Robert L. Bowne.

Robinson, Betsy, m. Shubael Bell.

Robinson, Lieut. Edward. On Thursday evening, Lieut. E. R. to Miss Rachel How, daughter to Mr. John How. (S. Dec. 8, 1792.)

See Capt. James Robinson.

Robinson, Elizabeth, m. Thomas Alger.

Robinson, Capt. James. On Wednesday evening last, at Dorchester, Capt. J. R. to Miss Polly Withington, daughter to Mr. Samuel Withington; and on Thursday evening, Lieut. Edward Robinson to Miss Rachel How, daughter to Mr. John How. (S. Dec. 8, 1792.)

Robinson, Jane, m. Thomas Hodges.

Robinson, Mary, m. John Morton.

Robinson, Mary, m. Henry Sadler.

Robinson, William. W. R., Esq., merchant, of Philadelphia, to Miss Deliverance Doggett, of this town. (W. Feb. 15, 1786.)

Roby, Captain Joseph. In this town, Capt. J. R. to Mrs. Elizabeth Henry. (S. Nov. 7, 1789.)

Roby, Rev. Joseph. In this town, Rev. J. R. of Lynn, to Mrs. Zerniah Marston, of this town. (W. Aug. 8, 1792.)

Rodman, Charity, m. Thomas Rotch.

Rogers, Daniel, Jun. At Gloucester, Mr. D. R., Jun., to Miss Sally Saunders. (W. Sept. 26, 1792.)

Rogers, Esther, m. John Rowe.

Rogers, Capt. John. At Newbury-Port, Capt. J. R. to Miss Mary Stanwood, daughter to Capt. Joseph Stanwood. (W. Feb. 6, 1793.)

Rogers, Lovey, m. James Burtwell.

Rogers, Polly, m. Henry Stimpson.

Rogers, Sally, m. Francis Mallet.

Rogers, Thomas. Mr. T. R., merchant, to Miss Abigail Bridge. (W. Nov. 5, 1788.)

Rogerson, Dr. Robert. Dr. R. R. to Miss Lucy Dearing. (W. March 30, 1785.)

Rogerson, Thomas. At Providence, Mr. T. R., of Alexandria, merchant, to Miss Anstis Olney. (W. Aug. 22, 1792.)

Rolf, Polly, m. Capt. Thomas Morris.

Rolfe, Paul. In this town, Mr. P. R., A.B., of New-Concord, to Miss Elizabeth Kirkwood, of this town. (S. Oct. 13, 1792.)

Root, James. [At Great Barrington] Mr. J. R. to Mrs. Abigail Pixley. (S. March 2, 1793.)

Ropes, Betsey, m. Jonathan Hodges.

Ropes, Jane, m. Capt. John T. Ropes.

Ropes, Capt. John T. At Salem, Capt. J. T. R. to Miss Jane Ropes. (S. Nov. 21, 1789.)

Ropes, Sally, m. Robert Bray.

Rose, Mary, m. Alexander Baker.

Rose, Polly, m. Caleb Francis.

Rose, Sally, m. Thomas Brisco.

Ross, Sarah, m. Edmund M. Blunt.

Ross, Thomas. [At New York] Mr. T. R. to Miss Ann Lions. (S. May 19, 1792.)

Rotch, Thomas. At Newport, Mr. T. R., merchant, of Nantucket, to Miss Charity Rodman, of that place. (W. May 19, 1790.)

Roulstone, John. Mr. J. R. to Miss Dolly Smith, . . . [both] of this town. (S. Oct. 23, 1790.)

Round, Capt. John. In this town, Capt. J. R. to Miss Hitty Clark. (W. June 14, 1786.)

Rouse, Joseph. In this town, Mr. J. R. to Miss Mehitable Cabot, both of this town. (W. Aug. 14, 1793.)

Rouselet, Nicholas Gysburtus. On Tuesday, the 27th ult., at Portsmouth, by the Rev. Joseph Buckminster, Mr. N. G. R., of this town, to Miss Elizabeth Catherine Mossatt, of Portsmouth. (W. April 4, 1787.)

Row, Betsy, m. Fisher Gay.

Rowe, John. At Gloucester, J. R., Esq. to Miss Esther Rogers, both of that place. (W. May 9, 1792.)

Rowland, Capt. Jonathan. [At New York] Capt. J. R. to Miss Cornelia Warner. (S. May 19, 1792.)

Royse, John. At New York, Mr. J. R. to Miss Lydia Bull, of Hartford. (S. Nov. 10, 1792.)

Ruggles, Miss, m. Nathaniel Scott.

Ruggles, Martha, m. Rev. John Fairfield.

Ruggles, Nathaniel. By the Rev. Mr. Clark, Mr. N. R., of Roxbury, to Miss Sally Fellows, of this town. (W. Nov. 8, 1786.)

Ruggles, Samuel. [In this town] Mr. S. R., merchant, to Miss Polly Blake. (S. Apr. 19, 1794.)

Rumrill, Thomas. Mr. T. R. to Miss Abigail Richardson. (W. Nov. 27, 1793.)

At Roxbury implied.

Rumsey, Nancy, m. Samuel Hichborn.

Runey, John. At Charlestown, Mr. J. R. to Miss Polly Turner. (S. July 1, 1786.)

Russell, Miss, m. Edward Cary, Jun.

Russell, Betsey, m. Capt. Stevens.

Russell, Capt. Edward. Capt. E. R., of Salem, to Miss Sally McClure, of this town. (S. June 16, 1792.)

Russell, Elijah. At Concord, Mr. E. R., editor of the "Mirrour," to Miss Polly Davis, of that town. (W. May 14, 1794.

Russell, Maj. Ephraim. At Princeton, Maj. E. R., of Stow, to Miss Eunice Merrick, of that place. (S. Feb. 18, 1792.)

Russell, John. At Philadelphia, Mr. J. R., of Boston, printer, to Miss Eliza Milne, daughter of Mr. Edmund Milne, of that city. (W. April 17, 1793.)

Russell, Mary, m. Isaac Winslow, Jun.

Russell, Mrs. Mary, m. William Doggett.

Russell, Seth. At Northampton, Mr. S. R. to Miss Polly Ewerson. (W. Oct. 29, 1794.)

Russell, Thomas. At Plymouth, T. R., Esq., of this town, to Miss Betsy Watson, daughter of George Watson, Esq., of that place. (W. Nov. 19, 1788.)

Rust, Susannah, m. Capt. Alexander Nichels.

Rutter, Ann, m. Isaac Burneston.

Sadler, Henry. In Savannah, Mr. H. S. to Miss Mary Robinson. (S. Mar. 3, 1792.)

Safford, William. At Salem, Mr. W. S. to Miss Abigail Swansey. (S. June 16, 1792.)

Salisbury, Wait, m. William Wentworth Fernald.

Salmon, John. By the Rev. Mr. Eliot, Mr. J. S. to Miss Betsey Sestren. (W. Jan. 4, 1792.)

Salmon, Polly, m. Andrew Brimmer.

Salter, Jenny, m. Capt. Joseph Ingraham.

Saltonstall, Rebecca, m. Peter Christopher.

Sample, Ann, m. William Grant.

Sanders, Miss, m. K. K. Van Rensselear.

Sands, Benjamin. [At New York] Mr. B. S., late of Boston, to Miss Peggy Michaels. (S. Nov. 10, 1792.)

Sanford, Miss, m. James Dwight.

Sanford, Bathsheba, m. Rev. Ethan Smith.

Sanford, Clarissa, m. Rev. John Morse.

Saphum, Mrs. Sally, m. David Stetson.

Sargeant, John. In this town, Mr. J. S. to Miss Sally Larkin, both of this town. (W. May 19, 1790.)

Sargent, Catharine, m. Theodore Jones.

Sargent, Winthrop. In the western territory, W. S., Esq., Secretary of that territory, to Miss Tupper, daughter to Gen. Tupper. (W. May 27, 1789.)

Saunders, Daniel. At Salem, Mr. D. S. to Miss Sally Gill. (S. Oct. 25, 1794.)

Saunders, Sally, m. Daniel Rogers, jun.

Saunders, Sally, m. Thomas Augustus Vernon.

Savage, Elizabeth, m. John Cooper.

Savens, Abijah. At Newtown, Mr. A. S. to Miss Sukey Wenchester. (S. Apr. 28, 1792.)

Sawyer, John. [At Portsmouth] Mr. J. S. to Miss Sally Stagpole. (S. Sept. 20, 1794.)

Saxon, William. Mr. W. S., merchant, to Mrs. Mary Wheeler. (W. Jan. 8, 1794.)

Schuyler, Jeremiah. [At Albany] Mr. J. S., of Warrensbush, to Miss Jane Cutler. (W. Mar. 20, 1793.)

Scollay, Mary, m. Rev. Mr. Prentiss.

Scott, Betsy, m. Dr. Abijah Cheever.

Scott, Catharine, m. Capt. John Andrews.

Scott, Daniel. In this town, Mr. D. S., merchant, to Miss Betsy Holmes, both of this town. (W. Dec. 26, 1792.)

Scott, Hannah, m. William Barton.

Scott, James. At New York, Mr. J. S., merchant, to Miss Elizabeth C. Sowers. (W. Feb. 20, 1793.)

Scott, Nancy, m. Nathaniel Patten.

Scott, Nathaniel. At the Court House, yesterday, Mr. N. S. to Miss Ruggles, both belonging to adjacent towns. (W. July 3, 1793.)

The circumstances of the marriage are described in eighteen lines following the above notice. He preferred marriage to remaining in jail.

Scott, Peggy, m. Samuel Cobb.

Scott, Peter C. [In this town] Mr. P. C. S. to Miss Susanna Homans. (S. May 24, 1794.)

Seabury, Betsy, m. Ammi C. Hall.

Seabury, Hannah, m. John Jarvis.

Sears, David. At Providence, Mr. D. S., of this town, merchant, to Miss Winthrop, daughter of John Stille Winthrop, Esq., of New London. (W. June 21, 1786.)

Seaver, Samuel. [At Wiscasset] Mr. S. S. to Miss Hannah Smith. (W. Jan. 8, 1794.)

Seaver, William. In this town, Mr. W. S. to the engaging Miss Susannah Blake. (W. Nov. 14, 1787.)

Seavey, Sally, m. Joseph Dearborn.

Secomb, Betsy, m. John Hall.

Selsbry, Polly, m. Caleb Loring.

Sene, Col. At New York, Col. S., of S. Carolina (of the late American Army), to Miss Van Berckel, of that city, daughter of His Excellency Mr. Van Berckel, late Minister of the United Netherlands to the United States of America. (W. June 13, 1792.)

Seney, Hon. Joshua. At New York, Hon. J. S., Member of Congress, to Miss Fanny Nicholson, of that city. The Miss Nicholson's have been very fortunate — in attracting the attention of the Rulers of the Nation. — One of them was some time since married to the Most Hon. William Few, of the Senate — and another, we are told, is now addressed by a very worthy member from Virginia. Nor are these ladies more fortunate than meritorious. S. May 15, 1790.)

Serrat, Abigail, m. Hugh Pebbles.

Sessions, Thomas. At Newport, Mr. T. S. to Miss Betsy Marchant, daughter to the Hon. Henry Marchant, Esq., of that city. (S. Nov. 5, 1791.)

Sestren, Betsey, m. John Salmon.

Seton, Miss, m. Hon. John Vining.

Seton, James. At New York, Mr. J. S., merchant, to Miss Mary Hoffman, daughter of Nicholas Hoffmann, Esq., of that city. (W. Apr. 4, 1792.)

Sewall, Hon. David. The Hon. D. S., Esq., Federal Judge of the District of Maine, to Miss Elizabeth Langdon, eldest daughter of the Rev. Dr. Langdon, late President of the University of Cambridge. (S. Dec. 18, 1790.)

Sewall, Hannah, m. Martin Cushing.

Sewall, Henry. [At Bath, Kennebeck] Mr. H. S. to Miss Esther Wheeler Moody. (W. Nov. 12, 1794.)

Sewall, Joseph. At Bath, Kennebeck, Mr. J. S. to Miss Lydia Marsh. (W. Nov. 12, 1794.)

Sewall, Samuel. [At Bath, Kennebeck] Mr. S. S. to Miss Polly Lambert. (W. Nov. 12, 1794.)

Seward, Benjamin. In this town, Mr. B. S. to Miss Rebecca Peete. (W. July 22, 1789.)

Seymore, Mrs. Bridget, m. John Whitney.

Shackerly, Capt. John H. [At New York] Capt. J. H. S. to Miss Elizabeth Kumbel. (W. June 13, 1792.)

Shaffer, Barnet. At Philadelphia, Mr. B. S. to the amiable Miss Sophia Springer, aged 13 years and 9 months. (S. Oct. 27, 1787.)

Shafton, Capt. Capt. S., of London, to the amiable Miss Polly Vincent, of this town. (S. March 9, 1793.)

Shattuck, Capt. Jeremiah. At Pepperel, Capt. J. S., aged 90, to Mrs. Ruth Bixby, aged 75; his descendants are 10 children, 60 grandchildren, about 70 great-grandchildren, and 1 of the 5th generation — her descendants are 13 children, 39 grandchildren, &c. (S. March 10, 1792.)

Shaw, Benjamin. At New York, Mr. B. S., of Boston, to Miss Charity Smith, of the former place. (S. Nov. 22, 1794.)

Shaw, Betsy, m. Andrew Craigie.

Shaw, Rev. Josiah Crocker. At Marshfield, Rev. J. C. S., of Cohasset, to Miss Ruth Stockbridge Winslow, daughter to Isaac Winslow, Esq. (W. Mch. 27, 1793.)

Shaw, Samuel. In this town, by the Rev. Mr. Eckley, S. S., Esq., to Miss Hannah Phillips. (W. Aug. 29, 1792.)

Shaw, Temperance, m. Joseph Blish.

Shaw, William. In this town, W. S., Esq., to Miss Proctor, eldest daughter of Edward Proctor, Esq. (W. Oct. 21, 1789.)

Shaw, Rev. William. The Rev. W. S., of Marshfield, to Miss Nancy Checkley, of this town. (W. Oct. 6, 1790.)

Sheaffe, Nancy, m. John Erving, jun.

Shepard, Mrs., m. Samuel Hunt.

Shepard, Allice, m. Abiel Winship.

Shephard, Rev. Mase. In this town, the Rev. M. S., of Little Compton, Rhode Island, to Miss Deborah Haskins, daughter of Capt. John Haskins, distiller. (W. July 9, 1788.)

Married July 6. Haskins' R. W. Emerson; his maternal ancestors, p. 147.

Shepherd, Nancy, m. Joseph Edmunds.

Shepherd, Polly, m. Benjamin Wheeler.

Sherburne, John Samuel. At Portsmouth, J. S. S., Esq., to Miss Submit Boyd, daughter to the Hon. George Boyd, Esq., deceased. (S. Nov. 5, 1791.)

Sherburne, Joseph. In this town, J. S., Esq., late from India, to Miss Frances Johnstone Dana, daughter to the Rev. Edmond Dana, D.D., of Shrewsbury, England, and niece of the Hon. Chief Justice of this Commonwealth. (W. Nov. 20, 1793.)

Shields, Mrs., m. Hon. Henry Innes.

Shipman, Capt. Richard E. [In this town] Capt. R. E. S., of Hull (England), to Miss Mary Goodhue, only daughter of the late Dr. Goodhue. (W. Dec. 26, 1792.)

Shrewsbury, Earl of. At Bourdeaux (France), the Right Hon. the Earl, J. S., to Miss Hoy, of Dublin. The newly betrothed Countess of Shrewsbury is the daughter of Mr. Hoy, a stationer, in Dublin. [Nothing important follows.] (W. Feb. 13, 1793.)

Burke says Elizabeth, daughter of James Hoey.

Shuttleworth, Rev. Samuel. Rev. S. S., of Windsor, Vermont, to Miss Ames, sister of the Hon. Fisher Ames, Esq. (W. Jan. 18, 1792.)

Sibley, Polly, m. Joel Johnson.

Siders, Martin. In this town, Mr. M. S. to Miss Sally Cotton. (S. Feb. 21, 1789.)

Sigourney, Charles. Tuesday evening, Mr. C. S., of this town, merchent, to Miss Polly Greenleaf, of Newbury Port. (S. Sept. 27, 1788.)

Sigourney, Polly B., m. John Cathcart.

Silsby, Dorcas, m. Benjamin Smith.

Simmons, Micah. At Weymouth, Mr. M. S., of Dorchester, to Mrs. Abigail Webb, of Weymouth. (S. Apr. 19, 1794.)

Simmons, Thomas. In this town, by the Rev. Mr. Thacher, on Sunday evening last, Mr. T. S. to Miss Sally Low. (W. Nov. 23, 1791.)

Simms, Miss, m. Hon. Paul Carrington.

Simpkins, Rev. John. At Harwich, Rev. J. S. to Miss Olive Stone, of that place. (S. Sept. 8, 1792.)

Simpson, Abigail, m. John Foble.

Simpson, Mrs. Martha, m. Hon. James Sullivan.

Simpson, Nancy, m. Benjamin Burnet.

Simpson, Patty, m. Nathaniel Torrey.

Simpson, Sally, m. John Smith.

Sinclair, Isabella, m. Capt. Benjamin Bowland.

Singleton, George, jr. By the Rev. Mr. Eliot, Mr. G. S., jr., to Miss Lydia Gilbert Harris, both of this town. (W. Dec. 28, 1791.)

Singleton, James Carter. [In this town] Mr. J. C. S. to Miss Hannah Galley [Calley?]. (W. Oct. 30, 1793.)

Sisson, Edward. At Dedham, Mr. E. S. to Miss Nancy Fales, both of that place. (W. Oct. 16, 1793.)

Skillings, Mrs., m. Rev. James Lyon.

Skillings, Richard. Mr. R. S. to Miss Mary Cox. (S. Nov. 8, 1788.)

In 1764, May 11, Richard Skellings m. Mary Box.—Bridgman King's Chapel inscr., p. 308.

Slewman, Andrew. At Salem, Capt. A. S. to Miss Polly Elrins. (W. Oct. 18, 1786.)

Sloan, Katy, m. John M'Auly.

Sloo, Rachel, m. Peter Thompson.

Smith, Miss, m. Tobias Butler.

Smith, Mr. In this town, Mr. S. to Miss Whitterfield. (S. Sept. 6, 1794.)

Smith, Rev. Mr. [At Sandwich] Rev. Mr. S., of Chilmark, to Miss Nancy Williams. (S. Nov. 7, 1789.)

Smith, Abigail, m. Edward Dexter.

Smith, Allen. [At Taunton] Mr. A. S. to Miss Betsy Cobb, daughter to the Hon. David Cobb, Esq. (W. Aug. 13, 1788.)

Smith, Mrs. Ann, m. John Kettle.

Smith, Benjamin. In this town, Mr. B. S. to Miss Dorcas Silsby. (S. Aug. 28, 1790.)

Smith, Betsy, m. Samuel Tufts.

Smith, Bridget, m. Abel Bartlett.

Smith, Bulah, m. Zadock French.

Smith, Charity, m. Benjamin Shaw.

Smith, Dolly, m. John Roulstone.

Smith, Rev. Ethan. [At Medway, west precinct] Rev. E. S., of Haverhill (N.H.), to Miss Bathsheba Sanford. (S. March 2, 1793.)

See also Rev. John Morse.

Smith, Ezra. At New Bedford, Mr. E. S. to Miss Sukey Nye. (S. Nov. 9, 1793.)

Smith, Hannah, m. Charles Miller.

Smith, Hannah, m. Samuel Seaver.

Smith, Mrs. Hannah, m. Jedediah Tucker.

Smith, Isaac. Mr. I. S., of Boston, to Miss Charity Houghton, of Milton. (W. Apr. 7, 1790.)

Smith, Isaac, jr. Mr. I. S., jr., of Charlestown, to Miss Prudence Newell, of this town. (W. Jan. 11, 1792.)

Smith, Rev. John. The Rev. J. S., of Hanover, to the amiable Miss Sukey Mason, second daughter of Col. David Mason, of this town. (W. Jan. 19, 1785.)

Smith, John. Mr. J. S. to Miss Sally Simpson, both of this town. (S. June 8, 1793.)

Smith, Martha, m. James Blanton.

Smith, Dr. Oliver. Dr. O. S. to Miss Ann Coffin. (S. June 11, 1785.)

Smith, Rebecca, m. Samuel Blodget.

Smith, Rebecca, m. Matthew Bunce.

Smith, Ruth, m. Robert Boyd.

Smith, Sally, m. Dr. Ezra Hoyt.

Smith, Mrs. Sally, m. Elias Morgan.

Smith, Samuel. Mr. S. S. to Mrs. Abigail Pittengill, an agreeable young widow. (W. Dec. 22, 1790.)

Smith, Samuel. At Fitchburg, Mr. S. S., merchant, of Peterborough, to Miss Sally Garfield, of the former place (W. Nov. 27, 1793.)

Smith, Sarah, m. Isaac L. Kip.

Smith, Capt. Stephen. Capt. S. M., of Providence, to Miss Mary Dyer, of Boston. (W. Aug. 3, 1791.)

Smith, Hon. Thomas. At Barnstable, Hon. T. S., of Falmouth, to Mrs. Bacon. (W. Sept. 16, 1789.)

Smith, Thomas. At Newbury-Port, Mr. T. S. to Miss Sally Plumer. (W. July 5, 1794.)
Given July 2, as Plutner by mistake.

Smith, Thomas, jun. At Portland, Mr. T. S., jun., to Miss Polly Barker. (W. Sept. 19, 1792.)

Smith, William. On the 14th instant, at Newbury Port, by the Rev. Mr. Cary, Mr. W. S., of this town, merchant, to Miss Hannah Carter, eldest daughter of Nathaniel Carter, Esq., of that place. (M. June 25, 1787.)
In Boston Gazette.

Snell, Phebe, m. Abiel Tripp.

Snelling, Joseph. Mr. J. S. to Miss Elizabeth Warner. (S. June 28, 1794.)

Snelling, Samuel. Mr. S. S. to Miss Betsy Grant. (S. May 8, 1790.)

Snow, Clarissa, m. Dr. Daniel Stebbins.

Snow, Jacob. At New York, Mr. J. S. to Mrs. Sally Swain. (W. Nov. 12, 1794.)

Snow, John Crocker. At Falmouth, Mr. J. C. S. to Miss Polly Nickels. (S. June 14, 1794.)

Snow, Mrs. Margaret, m. Hon. Jethro Hussey.

Soden, Hannah, m. Rev. Nathaniel Lawrence.

Sohier, Edward. Mr. E. S. to Miss Davies [of this town]. (S. Sept. 30, 1786.)

Sollee, John. At Newport, J. S., Esq., of the Island of St. Domingo, to Miss Harriet Neyle, a young lady from South Carolina. (S. Nov. 2, 1793.)

Somes, John, jun. In this town, Mr. J. S., jun., to Miss Hannah Dilliway. (W. Sept. 25, 1793.)

Soper, Charlotte, m. Eli Hayden.

Soper, Rhoda, m. William Jones.

Soren, John. On Sunday evening last, Mr. J. S. to Miss Sally Johnson [both of this town]. (W. Oct. 15, 1794.)

Sowers, Elizabeth C., m. James Scott.

Spear, Benjamin. In this town, on Sunday evening last, Mr. B. S. to Miss Betsy Widerfield, both of this town. (W. June 27, 1792.)

Spear, Capt. David. Last Monday evening, Capt. D. S. to Mrs. Mary Holland. (W. May 4, 1791.)

Spear, David, Jun. At Eastham, on the 3d inst., Mr. D. S., jun., of this town, merchant, to Miss Mercy Higgins. (W. May 19, 1787.)

Spear, Hannah, m. Jeremiah Kahleer.

Spencer, Nathan. At Providence, Mrs. N. S., of East Greenwich, to Miss Ruth Anthony. (W. May 16, 1792.)

Spicer, Miss, m. Samuel Mongee.

Spir, Jesse. [In this town] Mr. J. S. to Miss Jenny Driver. (W. Jan. 1, 1794.)

Spooner, John. At Windsor (V.), Mr. J. S., of New-Bedford, printer, to Miss Isabella Patrick. (S. Sept. 21, 1793.)

Spooner, Rebecca, m. Jacob Cooper.

Spooner, Hon. Walter. At Newport, the Hon. W. S., Esq., of Bedford, in this State, to Mrs. Mary Peck, of Newport. (S. July 9, 1791.)

Spooner, Dr. William. Dr. W. S. to Miss Polly Phillips. S. Oct. 25, 1788.

Sprague, John. In this town, J. S., Esq., of Lancaster, to Mrs. Mary Ivers, widow of Thomas Ivers, Esq. (S. Dec. 22, 1787.)

Sprague, Joseph. In this town, Mr. J. S. to Miss Eliza Dowse, of Charlestown. S. Dec. 27, 1788.

Sprague, Samuel. [In this town] Mr. S. S. to Miss Deborah Wallace. (W. May 25, 1791.)

Spring, Dr. Marshall. At Philadelphia, Dr. M. S., of Watertown, in this State, to Mrs. Binney, of Philadelphia; an accomplished lady with an ample fortune. (W. Jan. 18, 1792.)

Deaths, W. Nov. 13, 1793: In Watertown, Mrs. Mary Spring, wife of Dr. Marshal Spring.

Springer, Sophia, m. Barnet Shaffer.

Stagpole, Sally, m. John Sawyer.

Stanton, John. At Charlestown, Mr. J. S. to Mrs. Mary Edes. (S. Nov. 23, 1793.)

Stanwood, Mary, m. Capt. John Rogers.

Star, Hannah, m. Birdsey Norton.

Starbuck, Levi. [At Nantucket] Mr. L. S. to Miss Betsey Ransdell. (S. Dec. 14, 1793.)

Starkweather, Mrs. Elizabeth, m. Hon. Reuben Bristor.

Starr, Betsy, m. Henry Pigeon.

Stead, Miss, m. Brigadier-General Pinckney.

Steaples, Cloe, m. Obadiah Woodward.

Stebbins, Dr. Daniel. At Springfield, Dr. D. S., of Longmeadow, to Miss Clarissa Snow, of Springfield. (S. June 4, 1791.)

Stebbins, Polly, m. Peletiah Bliss.

Stedman, William. W. S., Esq., of Lancaster, to Miss Almy Ellery, daughter to William Ellery, Esq., of Newport. (Nov. 3, 1790.)

Steele, Nancy, m. Silas Francis.

Stepson, Thomas. [In this town] Mr. T. S. to Miss Polly Harmond. (W. July 30, 1794.)

Stetson, David. [At Scituate] Mr. D. S. to Mrs. Sally Saphum. (W. Sept. 14, 1793.)

Stevens, Capt. At Charlestown, Capt. S. to Miss Betsey Russell, of that town. (W. Oct. 10, 1787.)

Stevens, Adonijah. At Redgbury, Mr. A. S. to Miss Polly Jones. (W. July 4, 1792.)

Stevens, Caroline, m. Capt: Caleb Hayden.

Stevens, Isaac. At Newburyport, Mr. I. S. to Miss Catharine Duteau. (S. Nov. 1, 1794.)

Stevens, Joanna, m. Jacob Foster.

Stevens, Mrs. Judith, m. John Murray.

Stevens, Dr. Simeon. At Bernardston, Dr. S. S. to Miss Eunice Cunnabell. (W. Dec. 11, 1793.)

Stevenson, Isabella, m. Joshua Thomas.

Stevenson, William. At Marblehead, Mr. W. S. to Miss Hannah Greely. (S. June 28, 1794.)

Stewart, Nancy, m. Daniel Allen.

Stickney, Mrs. Abigail, m. Capt. John Lyon, jun.

Stillman, Benjamin Morgan. Mr. B. M. S. to Miss Mary Balch. (S. Dec. 19, 1789.)

Stillman, Debby, m. Rev. Thomas Gray.

Stillman, Mary, m. Nathaniel Balch, jun.

Stimpson, Mrs. Catharine, m. James Ridgway.

Stimpson, Henry. [In this town] Mr. H. S. to Miss Polly Rogers. [W. Oct. 8, 1794.]

Stockton, F., m. Patrick Campbell, jun.

Stockwell, Daniel. At Westborough, Mr. D. S. to Miss Nancy Hazeltine. (W. Apr. 4, 1792.)

Stoddard, Polly, m. Ashbel Strong.

Stone, Dr. Dr. S., of Greenfield, to Miss Sally Banard. (S. Feb. 16, 1793.)

See also Capt. Joshua Clapp.

Stone, Betsy, m. Dr. Joseph Fisk, jun.

Stone, Eliza, m. David Hyslop.

Stone, Ethan. At Sandisfield, E. S., Esq., Attorney-at-Law, to Miss Polly Storrs. (S. Nov. 30, 1793.)

Stone, Hannah, m. Capt. Michael Lincoln.

Stone, Lucy, m. Nathaniel Green.

Stone, Mary, m. Joshua Nash.

Stone, Moses. [At Cumberland] Mr. M. S., of Waterford, to Miss Ruth Porter. (W. Feb. 12, 1794.)

Stone, Olive, m. Rev. John Simpkins.

Stone, Rebecca, m. Benjamin Faxon.

Stone, Sarah, m. Lemuel Ide.

Stone, Sarah, m. Lewis Keyes.

Stontenbourg, Eliza, m. Dr. Abraham Brewer.

Storrs, Polly, m. Ethan Stone.

Story, William, jun. At Philadelphia, Mr. W. S., jun., late of this town, to Miss Lydia Phillips, of that city. (S. Dec. 15, 1792.)

Stow, Edward. Mrs. E. S., of Philadelphia, to Miss Nancy B. Peck, of this town. (W. June 5, 1793.)

Stratford, Samuel. On Tuesday evening, by the Rev. Mr. Belknap, Mr. S. S. to Miss Lucy Wallcut. (S. Aug. 7, 1790.)

Street, Alice, m. Mace Tisdale.

Stretch, Joseph. At Philadelphia, J. S., Esq., to Miss Matlack, daughter to Timothy Matlack, Esq. (S. Feb. 25, 1792.)

Strode, Capt. John. At Martinsburg (Virg.), Capt. J. S., of the mature age of 78, to Miss Betsey Frayatt, of blooming 16. — N. B. Capt. Strode is immensely rich. (S. Dec. 20, 1794.)

Strong, Ashbel. At Pittsfield, A. S., Esq., to Miss Polly Stoddard. (S. Dec. 15, 1792.)

Strong, Dorothy, m. Samuel Hinkley.

Strong, Rev. Jonathan. The Rev. J. S., of Braintree, to Miss Joanna Odiorne, daughter of Deacon Odiorne, of Exeter, New-Hampshire. (W. Nov. 17, 1790.)

Stutson, Christiani, m. Alexander Young.

Stutson, Polly, m. William Andrews.

Stutson, Sally Ridgeway, m. Simeon Polley.

Stutson, Thomas. At Dedham, Mr. T. S., of this town, to Miss Matty Hadley, of that place. (W. March 7, 1792.)

Sullivan, Hon. James. At Portsmouth, on the 1st inst., the Hon. J. S., Esq., of this town, to Mrs. Martha Simpson, relict of the late Thomas Simpson, Esq., Commander of the continental frigate "Ranger." (W. Jan. 10, 1787.)

Sullivan, Mehitable, m. James Cutler.

Sumner, Alice, m. Thomas Howe.

Sumner, Benjamin. At Providence, Mr. B. S., tertius, of this town, to Miss Maria Green, of Coventry. (W. Jan. 9, 1788.)

Sumner, Betsey, m. Lieut. Jesse Goggett.

Sumner, Dea. Jabez. Dea. J. S., of Milton, to Miss Ruth Withington. (S. June 16, 1792.)

Sumner, Sally, m. George Homer.

Sumner, Samuel. By the Rev. Dr. Thatcher, Mr. S. S. to Miss Martha Barrett, daughter of Hon. Samuel Barrett. (S. Feb. 15, 1794.)

Sumner, Susannah, m. James Ridgway.

Sutherd, Abigail, m. John Foster.

Swain, Joshua. Mr. J. S. to Miss Eunice Wyer. (S. Dec. 7, 1793.)

At Nantucket?

Swain, Phebe, m. Tristram Barnard.

Swansey, Abigail, m. William Safford.

Sweet, Cynthia, m. Jonathan Gladding.

Sweet, Rufus. At South-Kingston, Mr. R. S. to Miss Betsy Clark. (S. Apr. 28, 1792.)

Sweeting, Ann, m. Capt. Benjamin Page.

Sweetser, Henry. At Charlestown, by the Rev. Mr. Paine, Mr. H. S. to Mrs. Phebe Hatch, relict of the late Capt. Hatch, of Malden. (S. Jan. 20, 1787.)

Swett, Betsey, m. William Leach.

Swift, Henry. Mr. H. S. to Miss Sally Brown, [both] of this town. (S. Nov. 27, 1790.)

Swift, Stephen. Mr. S. S., of Watertown, to Miss Sally Cook, daughter of Capt. Phineas Cook, late of Newton. (W. Nov. 12, 1788.)

Switcher, Samuel. At Cambridge, by the Rev. Mr. Fisk, Mr. S. S., of Athol (Conn.), to Miss Hannah Moore, of Cambridge. (S. Oct. 27, 1792.)

Swords, James. At New-York, Mr. J. S., printer, to Miss Rachael Buskirk. (S. Oct. 4, 1794.)

Symes, Anna, m. Isaac Cazneau.

Symmes, James. At Watertown, Mr. J. S. to Miss Sally Harback. (S. Feb. 2, 1793.)

A virtuous lady he has got;
And Citizen *Elliot* ti'd the knot!

Symonds, Huldah, m. James Cutler.

Symonds, John. At Salem, Mr. J. S. to Miss Betsy Pickering. (W. Apr. 17, 1793.)

Taber, Phebe, m. Theodore Doty.

Taggart, John. At Philadelphia, Mr. J. T., merchant, to Mrs. Kitty Byrnes, both of that place. (S. Nov. 10, 1792.)

Tallman, Hannah, m. William Delano.

Talton, Sarah, m. Walter Weeks.

Tapley, Isaac. Mr. I. T. of Cambridge, to Miss Nancy Wayne, of this town. (S. Jan. 25, 1794.)

Tapley, Polly, m. Joseph Miller.

Tappan, Amos. At Portsmouth, Mr. A. T. to the amiable Miss Isabel Buckminster. (W. Aug. 24, 1791.)

Tappan, Cornecia, m. Adam Doll.

Tappan, James. At Gloucester, Mr. J. T. to Miss Nancy Choate. (S. Nov. 23, 1793.)

Tappan, Joshua. At Newbury-Port, Mr. J. T. to Miss Nancy Ford. (S. May 7, 1791.)

Tappan, Rebecca, m. William Edwards.

Tappan, Sarrah, m. Capt. Roberdeau.

Tarr, Sally, m. David Marston.

Tasker, Matthew. [In this town] Mr. M. T. to Miss Maria Hamblin. (W. Dec. 19, 1792.)

Tate, Hannah, m. John Hathaway.

Taylor, Chase. [At Salem] C. T., Esq., of Sandborton, Strafford-county, N. H., to Mrs. Sarah Elkins of that town. (S. Feb. 16, 1793.)

Taylor, Dan. At East-Springfield, Mr. D. T. to Miss Hermoine B. Campbell. (S. Oct. 13, 1792.)

Taylor, Daniel, jun. At Yarmouth, Mr. D. T., jun., to Miss Desire Thatcher. (S. Dec. 28, 1793.)

Taylor, William. By the Rev. Mr. Thacher, Mr. W. T. to Miss Sally Pierpont, of this town. (W. July 6, 1791.)

Taylor, William. At Southborough, Mr. W. T. to Miss Hannah Angier. (W. March 14, 1792.)

Telfair, Ann, m. Benjamin Franklin Timothy.

Temple, Miss, m. Thomas Lindal Winthrop.

Templeman, Catherine Lawless, m. John Callender.

Templeton, Sally, m. James Dunbar.

Thatcher, Nabby, m. Thomas Hale.

Thatcher, Desire, m. Daniel Taylor, jun.

Thaxter, Desire, m. Levi Lincoln.

Thaxter, Mrs. Elizabeth, m. James Carter.

Thaxter, John. At Haverhill, J. T., Esq., Attorney at law, to Miss Elizabeth Duncan. (W. Nov. 28, 1787.)

Thaxter, Samuel. [In this town] Mr. S. T. to Miss Polly Helyer. (S. June 16, 1792.)

Thayer, Abner. Mr. A. T. to Miss Perses Turner. (S. Oct. 30, 1790.)

Thayer, Eleonora, m. Elijah Thayer.

Thayer, Elijah. At Braintree, last Thursday evening, Mr. E. T. to Miss Eleonora Thayer. (S. May 15, 1790.)

Thayer, Samuel. Mr. S. T. to Miss Rachel Carey. (S. Apr. 18, 1789.)

Thomas, Daniel. On Thanksgiving eve, at Middleborough, Mr. D. T., merchant, of Taunton, to Miss Eliza Alden, of Middleborough. (S. Nov. 9, 1793.)

Sixteen lines of verse follow. The last two are:

May Fortune still her liberal board display,
And life continue a Thanksgiving Day!

Thomas, George. In this town, by the Rev. Mr. Murray, Mr. G. T. to Miss Sally Thurston, both of this town. (S. Feb. 8, 1794.)

Thomas, Happy, m. Enoch Morse.

Thomas, John. At Portsmouth, Mr. J. T. to Mrs. Sally Clear. (W. Sept. 14, 1793.)

Thomas, Joshua. J. T., Esq., of Plymouth, member of the Hon. House of Representatives from that town, to Miss Isabella Stevenson, of this town. (S. Oct. 21, 1786.)

Thomas, Joshua. On Sunday evening, by the Rev. Mr. Freeman, Mr. J. T., printer, to Mrs. Hannah Thompson, of this town. (W. Sept. 30, 1789.)

Thomas, Marianne, m. James R. Hutchins.

Thompson, Abigail, m. Daniel Oliver.

Thompson, Archibald. [At New York] Mr. A. T. to Miss Kitty Applegate. (S. Feb. 2, 1793.)

Thompson, E., m. William M'Crea.

Thompson, Ephraim. Mr. E. T. to Miss Polly Washburn. (S. Feb. 26, 1791.)

Thompson, Mrs. Hannah, m. Joshua Thomas.

Thompson, Jacob. At Charlestown, Mr. J. T., of Hamilton, to Miss Nancy Robbins of the former place. (S. Nov. 8, 1794.)

Thompson, Jacob, jun. At Beverly, Mr. J. T., jun., to Miss Betsey Buckman. (W. Feb. 27, 1793.)

Thompson, Jenny, m. William Barnes.

Thompson, John. Mr. J. T. of 68, to Miss Elizabeth Clulow of 81—taking the fourth wife. (W. Jan. 2, 1793.)

At Leak (Eng.) implied. See Thomas Pilsbury.

Thompson, Nancy, m. Hon. Elbridge Gerry.

Thompson, Capt. Nathan G. At Baltimore, Capt. N. G. T. to Miss Elizabeth Jackson. (S. Aug. 11, 1792.)

Thompson, Peter. At New York, Mr. P. T. to Miss Rachel

Sloo. (S. Apr. 7, 1792.)

Thompson, Ruthy, m. Thomas Bennet.

Thompson, Deacon Thomas. At Charlestown, Deacon T. T., of Newburyport, to Mrs. Sarah Wood, Charlestown. (W. Dec. 19, 1792.)

Thomson, Sally, m. George Thomas.

Thorlo, Polly, m. Stephen Wait.

Thorndike, John. At Concord, N. H., Mr. J. T. to Miss Dolly Wilson. (S. Apr. 7, 1792.)

Thorndike, Larkin. At Beverly, L. T., Esq., to Mrs. Jewitt, of Ipswich. (S. Jan. 14, 1792.)

Thornton, Elizabeth, m. Edward Wade.

Throop, Mrs. Abigail, m. Capt. John Arnold.

Thurber, Sally, m. George Benson.

Thurston, Joanne, m. Capt. Simon Wiggen.

Thwing, James. Mr. J. T., cashier of the Massachusetts Bank, to Miss Jannet Love. (W. Nov. 13, 1793.)

Thwing, Capt. Nathaniel. [In this town] Capt. N. T. to Miss Mary Greenleaf. (S. Aug. 16, 1794.)

Tichenor, Elisha. [In this town] Mr. E. T. to Mrs. Betsey Curtiss. (W. May 26, 1790.)

Tilden, Betsey, m. George Blanchard.

Tilden, Joanne, m. Dr. Galen Otis.

Tileston, Ebenezer. Mr. E. T., to Miss Sarah Marson. (S. Dec. 18, 1790.)

Tileston, Esther, m. A. Clapp.

Tileston, Lemuel. [In this town] Mr. L. T., to Miss Polly Minns. (S. Feb. 7, 1789.)

Tileston, Lucy, m. Samuel Withington.

Tileston, Capt. Thomas. At Roxbury, Capt. T. T. to the amiable Miss Betsy Wait. (S. July 10, 1790.)

Tilley, Betsey, m. Peter Butterfield.

Tilton, Catherine, m. Nathaniel Parker.

Tilton, Lucy, m. David Lincoln.

Tilton, Rachel, m. Barnabas Knox.

Timothy, Benjamin Franklin. At Philadelphia, Mr. B. F. T., of Charleston, S. C., to Miss Ann Telfair. (S. June 22, 1793.)

Tisdale, Mace. At Quincy, a newly incorporated town in this county, by the Rev. Anthony Wibird, Mr. M. T., of Easton, to Miss Alice Street. (S. March 3, 1792.)

Titcomb, Eliza, m. Ebenezer Gullishan.

Toby, Capt. Lemuel. Capt. L. T., to the amiable Miss Patty Williams, daughter of the late Rev. Abraham Williams, of Sandwich. (W. July 18, 1787.)

Todd, Mrs., m. Hon. James Madison.

Tolman, Sally, m. Abraham Williams.

Torrey, Deborah, m. Gershom Cutter.

Torrey, Joseph. Mr. J. T. of Worcester, to Miss Betsy Gendell, of this town. (S. Oct. 11, 1788.)

Torrey, Capt. Joseph. At Worcester, Capt. J. T. to Mrs. Azubah Goulding. (W. Dec. 24, 1794.)

Torrey, Nathaniel. [In this town] Mr. N. T. to Miss Patty Simpson. (June 18, 1791.)

Torrey, Sally, m. Capt. Ezekial Burroughs.

Torrey, Samuel. Last Thursday evening, Mr. S. T., merchant, to Miss Katy Gore, youngest daughter of John Gore, Esq., of this town. (W. July 5, 1786.)

Toscan, Jean. At Portsmouth, the Hon. le Sieur J. T., Vice-Consul of France, to Miss Elizabeth Parrot. (S. Dec. 18, 1790.)

Totman, Samuel. At South Hadley, Mr. S. T. to Mrs. Hannah Johnson. (S. Nov. 1, 1794.)

Tower, Lydia, m. Ebenezer Delano.

Towne, Gen. At Charleston, Gen. T. to Mrs. Sabra Coman, of Dudley. (W. Feb. 22, 1792.)

Townsend, John. [At New York] Mr. J. T. to Miss Rebecca Franklin. (S. Feb. 2, 1793.)

Townsend, Judith, m. Elijah Adams.

Townsend, Nabby, m. Edward Hall.

Townsend, Polly, m. Capt. Robert Pearce.

Townshend, Polly, m. Nathaniel Frothingham.

Tracy, Peleg. At Norwich, Mr. P. T to Miss Hannah Leffingwell. (S. Nov. 23, 1793.)

Tracy, Mrs. Sally, m. Capt. John Newson.

Trask, Mrs., m. S. Low.

Trask, Elijah. At Lexington, Mr. E. T. of Boston, to Miss Sally Benny. (W. Sept. 18, 1793.)

Trask, Jonathan. [In this town] Mr. J. T., wheelwright, to Miss Hannah Pelfrey [Palfrey?]. (W. May 23, 1792.)

Trask, Matilde, m. Edwin Locke.

Trask, Patty, m. Samuel Allen.

Treadwell, Rev. John. Rév. J. T., of Ipswich, to Mrs. Dorothy Goodhue, of that town. (W. July 25, 1787.)

Treet, Samuel. S. T., Esq., to Miss Nancy May. (S. June 26, 1790.)

Treferen, James. [In this town] Mr. J. T. to Mrs. Mary Mountford. (S. Feb. 11, 1792.)

Tremain, J. jun. At Halifax, Mr. J. T., jun., to Miss Lee. (S. Nov. 23, 1793.)

Trescot, Sally, m. Samuel Patson.

Trindle, Mrs., m. William Gilson.

Trindle, Betsy, m. William Gilson, jun.

Trip, Abrahàm, At Westport, Mr. A. T. to Miss Polly Warren. (W. Aug. 14, 1793.)

Tripe, Maria, m. Lemuel Barker.

Tripp, Abiel. At Westport, Mr. A. T. to Miss Phebe Snell. (S. Jan. 11, 1794.)

Trott, Elizabeth, m. Capt. Ephraim Wales.

Trow, Hannah, m. Nathan Foster.

Trueman, John. Mr. J. T. to Miss Sukey Casay. (Feb. 17, 1790.)

Tuck, Capt. Moses. [In this town] Capt. M. T. to Miss Sally Hagger, daughter of Mr. William G. Hagger, of this town. (W. Jan. 8, 1794.)

Tuck, Samuel Jones. At Nantucket, Mr. S. J. T., of this town, to Miss Judith Gardner, of that town. S. Dec. 17, 1791.

Tucker, Jedediah. At Shrewsbury, Mr. J. T., aged 78, to Mrs. Hannah Smith, aged 77. W. Dec. 1, 1790. See also John Rice.

Tucker, John. Mr. J. T., clerk of the Supreme Judicial Court, to the agreeable Miss Sally Henshaw, second daughter of Capt. Job Prince, Sen. S. Mch. 19, 1785.

Tucker, Capt. John. At Salem, Capt. J. T. to Miss Sally Mansfield, daughter of Mr. Matthew Mansfield. W. June 26, 1793.

Tucker, Mary, m. Joseph Dickman.

Tucker, Mrs. Peggy, m. Isaac Very.

Tucker, Polly, m. James Fisher.

Tucker, Susannah, m. Major Ziba Blake.

Tuckerman, Hannah, m. John Lopans.

Tuckerman, Lucretia, m. Robert Wyer, Jun.

Tufts, Amos. At Charlestown, Mr. A. T. to Miss Dabby Frothingham, both of that town. S. Aug. 19, 1786.

Tufts, Hon. Cotton. At Gloucester, Hon. C. T., of Weymouth, to Miss Warner. S. Nov. 7, 1789.

Tufts, Cotton, Jun. At Medford, Mr. C. T., Jun., merchant, of Weymouth, to Miss Mercy Brooks of Medford. W. Mch. 12, 1788.

Tufts, Lydia, m. Rev. Robert Gray.

Tufts, Samuel. Mr. S. T. to Miss Betsy Smith. W. June 27, 1792.

Tufts, Simon. At Medford, Mr. S. T. of Medford, to Miss Susanne Cox, of this town, daughter to Mr. Lemuel Cox, artist. W. Nov. 20, 1793.

Tupper, Miss, m. Winthrop Sargent.

Turell, Samuel. In this town, Mr. S. T. to Miss Polly Cutter. W. Jan. 14, 1789.

Turnbull, Nancy, m. Francis Osborne.

Turner, Barker. [At Nantucket] Mr. B. T. to Miss Susannah Pinkham. W. Oct. 23, 1793.

Turner, Betsey, m. Daniel Lathrop.

Turner, Perses, m. Abner Thayer.

Turner, Polly, m. John Runey.

Turnock, Mary, m. Thomas Pilsbury.

Turrell, Sukey, m. Edward Gray.

Tuttle, Daniel. Last Sunday, Mr. D. T. to Miss Polly Mason, daughter of Col. David Mason. S. Nov. 29, 1788.

Tuttle, Hannah, m. John Daniels.

Tuttle, Joseph. [In this town] Mr. J. T. to Miss Wells. S. Nov. 8, 1794.

Twentyman, B. In Virginia, Mr. B. T., aged 70, to Miss Betty Nutty, aged 50. S. Feb. 27, 1790.

Tyler, Amasa. [At Great Barrington] Mr. A. T. to Miss Hannah White. S. Mch. 2, 1793.

Tyler, David. Mr. D. T., goldsmith, to Miss Sally Wheelwright, daughter of Capt. Job Wheelwright. S. Dec. 31, 1785.

Tyler, Hannah Luther, m. Samuel Pierce.

Tyng, Dudley Atkins. In this town, D. A. T., of Tyngsborough, to Miss Sally Higginson, daughter of Stephen Higginson, Esq., of this town. S. Oct. 27, 1792.

Umberfield, Mrs., m. N. Woodrnff.

Underwood, John. At Baltimore, Mr. J. U. to Miss Elizabeth Davis. W. May 23, 1792.

Underwood, Polly, m. Elisha Ellis.

Underwood, Mrs. Sally, m. Edward Blake.

Urann, Betsey, m. Samuel Andrews.

Vallance, Mary, m. Horatio Gates.

Van Berckel, Miss, m. Col. Sene.

Vandegret, Elizabeth, m. John Albro.

Van Deren, Miss, m. George Johnson.

Vanderspeigel, Margaret Van Vauxter, m. Jonathan Dwight.

Van Deuser, Sally, m. Joseph Hitchcock.

Van Horne, Cornelia m. Hon. Philip Livingston.

Van Rensselear, Betsy, m. Peter Ed. Elmendorph.

Van Rensselear, K. K. At Albany, K. K. V. R., Esq., to Miss Sanders. W. Feb. 16, 1791.

Vaughan, Charles. By the Rev. Doctor Parker, on Thursday the 7th instant, C. V., Esq., to Miss Frances Western Apthorp. S. July 9, 1791.

Veasie, Rachel, m. Thomas Hilton.

Vernon, Thomas Augustus. Mr. T. A. V. of St. Petersburg, Russia, to Miss Sally Saunders. W. June 4, 1788.

Veron, Stephen. Mr. S. V. to Miss Abial Holland. S. Dec. 1, 1787.

Verry, Nancy, m. Elijah Wiswal.

Very, Isaac. At Salem, Mr. I. V. to Mrs. Peggy Tucker. W. May 16, 1792.

Vialli, Mrs. Elizabeth, m. Nathaniel Wheaton.

Viburt, Hannah, m. William Morgan.

Vickary, Samuel. Mr. S. V. to Miss Rebecca Parker. W. Feb. 22, 1786.

Vickery, Capt. David. At Taunton, Capt. D. V to Miss Priscilla Barnum, both of that town. W. Dec. 31, 1794.

Viebart, Sally, m. James Gummer.

Vinal, John. At Watertown, Mr. J. V. to Miss Sukey Adams, of this town. W. Apr. 24, 1793.

Vinall, Charlotte, m. Maj. Ebenezer Kent.

Vincent, Polly, m. Capt. Shafton.

Vincent, Thomas. In Salem, Mr. T. V. to Miss Hannah Cloutman. W. Apr. 25, 1792.

Vining, Hon. John. At New York, the Hon. J. V., Esq., Representative in Congress, from the State of Delaware, to Miss Seton, daughter to William Seton, Esq. S. Dec. 11, 1790.

Vischer, Gerrit G. At Albany, Mr. G. G. V. to Miss Rebecca Brooks. S. Nov. 23, 1793.

Voax. Hannah, m. Hezekiah Chadwick.

Vose, Lucy, m. Gregory Clark.

Wade, Edward. In Virginia, 27th ult. Mr. E. W. to Mis Elizabeth Thornton, whose courtship began 57 years since. S. Sept. 26, 1789.

Wainwright, Nabby, m. John Carver, Jun.

Wait, Betsy, m. Capt. Thomas Tileston.

Wait, Ruthy, m. Thomas Read.

Wait, Stephen. At Portland, Mr. S. W., to Miss Polly Thorlo, both of that town. S. March 5, 1791.

Waite, Betsy, m. Capt. James Codman.

Walcutt, Capt. Benjamin. Capt. B. W. to Miss Betsy Hawes. S. Aug. 15, 1789.

Waldo, Samuel. Mr. S. W., merchant, to Miss Sally Tyng Winslow. S. Feb. 14, 1789.

Waldren, Joseph. In this town, Mr. J. W. to Miss Nancy Roach. S. Jan. 15, 1791.

Wales, Capt. Ephraim. Capt. E. W. to Miss Elizabeth Trott, of this town. S. Apr. 4, 1789.

Walker, Dudley. [In this town?] Mr. D. W., merchant of this town, to Miss Elinora Clark, of Milton. S. May 12, 1792.

Walker, Jane, m. Nathaniel Ward.

Wallace, Deborah, m. Samuel Sprague.

Wallace, Elizabeth, m. Levy Clap.

Wallace, Mrs. Sally, m. George Richards.

Wallcut, Lucy, m. Samuel Stratford.

Walley, Sally, m. John Phillips.

Wallis, Elizabeth, m. Capt. Joseph Ripley.

Walter, William. In this town, by the Rev. Dr. Walter, Mr. W. W., merchant, to Miss Sally Bicker. S. Apr. 26, 1794.

Ward, Betsy, m. Benjamin Corey.

Ward, Andrew. At Salem, Mr. A. W. to Miss Patty Babbidge. W. Jan. 23, 1793.

Ward, Artemas, Jun. At Weston, A. W., Jun., Esq., to Miss Catharine Maria Dexter. S. Dec. 27, 1788.

Ward, George C. At Salem, Mr. G. C. W. to Miss Nabby Elkins, both of that town. S. June 10, 1786.

Ward, Hannah, m. Mathias Day.

Ward, Nathaniel. At Wilmington, N. C., Mr. N. W., of Salem, in this State, to Miss Jane Walker, of Wilmington. W. Apr. 13, 1791.

Ward, Sally, m. Benjamin Felt.

Ward, Sarah, m. Elijah Brigham.

Warden, Betsey, m. Samuel Creese.

Wardrobe, Capt. John. Capt. J. W. to Miss Nancy Wentworth, S. Dec. 18, 1790. [At Portsmouth implied.]

Warner, Miss, m. Hon. Cotton Tufts.

Warner, Mrs., m. John M. Lovell.

Warner, Betsey, m. Capt. Peleg Wood, Jun.

Warner, Cornelia, m. Capt. Jonathan Rowland.

Warner, Elizabeth, m. Joseph Snelling.

Warner, Hannah, m. Joseph Edmonds.

Warren, Abijah. Mr. A. W., of Attleboro', to Miss Lydia Nightingale, daughter of the late Samuel Nightingale, Esq. W. Oct. 30, 1793.

Warren, Betsy, m. Arnold Welles, Jun.

Warren, Henry. At Plymouth, Mr. H. W. to Miss Mary Winslow. S. Nov. 26, 1791.

Warren, Polly, m. Abraham Trip.

Warren, Sally, m. Jonathan Lander.

Washburn, Polly, m. Ephraim Thompson.

Washington, Corban. In Virginia, Mr. C. W., son of Col. John Augustine Washington, and nephew of the General, to Miss Hannah Lee, daughter of the Hon. Richard Henry Lee, Esq. S. June 9, 1787.

Washington, Mildred, m. Thomas Lee.

Waterbury, P. C. [At New York] Mr. P. C. W. to Miss Lydia Curtis. W. June 13, 1792.

Waterhouse, Dr. Benjamin. Dr. B. W., professor of the theory and practice of physick in the University of Cambridge, to Miss Elizabeth Oliver.

Watson, Betsy, m. Thomas Russell.

Watson, Elkanah. At Marblehead, Mr. E. W., of Plymouth, to Mrs. Glover, of Marblehead. W. Feb. 1, '92.

Watson, Ellen, m. John Davis.

Watts, Hannah, m. Capt. James Brown.

Watts, Hannah, m. David West.

Watts, Samuel. By the Rev. Dr. Stillman, Mr. S. W., to Miss Joanna Harden. W. Jan. 5, '91.

Wayne, Nancy, m. Isaac Tapley.

Weare, Nabby, m. Joseph Alexander.

Weaver, Betsey, m. John Greenwood.

Webb, Abigail, m. Capt. Henry Burbeck.

Webb, Abigail, m. Micah Simmons.

Webb, Deborah, m. Joseph Barrett, jun.

Webb, Martha, m. Matthew Dennison D'Orville.

Webb, Nathan. In this town, Mr. N. W., mer., to Miss Sally Leach, both of this town. S. July 19, '94.

Webb, Sally, m. Ebenezer Jénnison.

Webber, Joseph. Mr. J. W., tailor, to Miss Polly Winnet. W. Mch. 9, '85.

' When Worth unites in Virtue's band,
' The happiness to aye must stand.'

Webster, Hannah, m. Rev. John Foster.

Webster, Noah, jun. In this town, N. W., jun., Esq., of Hartford, to Miss Rebecca Greenleaf, daughter of William Greenleaf, Esq., of this town. W. Oct. 28, '89.

Webster, Polly, m. William D. Doak.

Webster, Dr. Redford. On Sunday evening, Doctor R. W., to Miss Hànnah White, daughter of Mr. John White. W. Sept. 5, '87.

Wedgery, William. In this town, W. W., Esq., of New Gloucester, to Mrs. Elizabeth Dafforne, of this town. S. Oct. 30, '90.

Weed, Mrs. Elizabeth, m. Dea. Jacob Burgiss.

Weeks, Walter. [At Portsmouth.] Mr. W. W., to Miss Sarah Talton. S. Nov. 22, '94.

Weiss, Lucy, m. John Wyeth.

Weld, Miss, m. Ebenezer T. Andrews.

Weld, Benjamin. On Sunday evening last, B. W., Esq., Deputy Collector of this District, to the amiable Miss Nabby Perkins, daughter of Col. William Perkins, Commandant at Castle Island. W. Sept. 12, '92.

Weld, Ezra Waldo. At Worcester, Mr. E. W. W., printer, of Springfield, to Miss Mary Wheeler, daughter of Joseph Wheeler, Esq. W. Apr. 7, '90.

Weld, Polly, m. William Morgan.

Welles, Arnold, jun. Last evening, Mr. A. W., jun., merchant, to the amiable Miss Betsy Warren, eldest daughter of the late General Warren. W. Sept. 7, '85.

Wells, Dea. At Roxbury, Dea. Wells, to the amiable Miss Childs. W. Sept. 18, '93.

Wells, Miss, m. Joseph Tuttle.

Wells, Ashbee, at Hartford, Mr. A. W., jun., to Miss Mary Hopkins. S. Oct. 4, '94.

Welsh, Betsey, m. Nathaniel Hancock.

Welsh, Ezra. At Charlestown, by the Rev. M. Morse, Mr. E. W., to Miss Rachel Mallett. W. Dec. 30, '89.

Welsh, Grace, m. Samuel Payson.

Welsh, Nancy, m. Daniel Butler.

Wench, Capt. At Wiscasset, Capt. W., to Miss Priscilla Ford. W. Jan. 8, '94.

Wenchester, Sukey, m. Abijah Savens.

Wentworth, Kezia, m. Joab Hunt.

Wentworth, Nancy, m. Capt. John Wardrobe.

Wesson, William. At Woburn, Mr. W. W., of this town, to Miss Polly Nevers, of that place. W. Sept. 19, '92.

West, David. In this town, last evening, Mr. D. W., to Miss Hannah Watts. W. Feb. 4, '89.

West, Francis. At Philadelphia, F. W., Esq., to Miss Nixon. W. Jan. 23, '93.

West, Sally, m. Asa Graham.

Western, Nathan. At Lincoln, Mr. N. W., to Miss Nancy Fox. W. Nov. 26, '88.

Whales, Joseph. At Lancaster, Mr. J. W., merchant, to Miss Eliza Willard, both of that place. W. Jan. 29, '94.

Wheaton, Caleb. In this town, Mr. C. W., to Miss Elizabeth Dall. S. Oct. 29, '91.

Wheaton, Joseph. At Halifax, Capt. J. W., to Miss Sally Fletcher, both of Rutland, in this Commonwealth. W. Sept. 6, '86.

Wheaton, Nathaniel. At Rehoboth, Mr. N. W., aged 66, to the amiable Mrs. Elizabeth Vialli, aged 56 years. W. June 6, '92.

Wheaton, Polly, m. Samuel Davis.

Wheeler, Miss, m. Abraham K. Whiting.

Wheeler, Benjamin. Last Thursday evening, by the Rev. Mr. Everet, Mr. B. W., merchant, to Miss Polly Shepherd [of this town]. S. Sept. 30, '86.

Wheeler, Eliza, m. Charles Groves.

Wheeler, Ephraim. At Norwich, Mr. E. W., of Montville, aged 77, to Miss Hitty Williams, aged 24. S. Mch. 17, '92.

Wheeler, Dr. John. At Menotomy, Dr. J. W., of Dover (N. H.), to Miss Rebeccah Harris, of Malden. S. Mch. 16, '93.

Wheeler, Capt. John. In this town, Capt. J. W., to Mrs. Goodenow. S. June 14, '94.

Wheeler, Mrs. Mary, m. William Saxon.

Wheeler, Mary, m. Ezra Waldo Weld.

Wheeler, Polly, m. William Wyman.

Wheeler, Sally, m. Barzillia Homes.

Wheeler, Samuel S. [In this town.] Mr. S. S. W., to Miss Faith Bass. S. Nov. 8, '94.

Wheeler, Thomas. Last Sunday evening, by the Rev. Mr. West, Mr. T. W., to the amiable Miss Massy Riggs. W. Feb. 1, '92.

Wheeler, William. In this town, Mr. W. W., to Miss Polly Jones. W. Nov. 28, '92.

Wheelock, Elizabeth, m. John Rice.

Wheelock, Kezia, m. Abijah Drury.

Wheelwright, Capt. Benjamin. In this town, Capt. B. W., to Miss Rebecca Gardner. S. May 31, '94.

Wheelwright, Lot. In this town, Mr. L. W., to Miss Susanna Wilson of Cambridge. S. Dec. 14, '93.

Wheelwright, Sally, m. David Tyler.

Wheston, Francis. [In this town] Mr. F. W., to Miss Elizabeth Downs. W. Mch. 13, '93.

Whipple, Amy, m. Henry Charles Jones.

Whipple, Hannah, m. Francis Blanchard.

Whipple, James, jun. At Grafton, Mr. J. W. jun., to Miss Sally Meriam. W. Dec. 19, '92.

Whipple, Polly, m. John Botang.

Whippy, Lucinda, m. John Hawkins.

Whiston, Obediah. [In this town] Mr. O. W., to Miss Isabella Dawes. S. Aug. 23, '94.

White, Miss, m. Bailey Bartlett.

White, Rev. Calvin. The Rev. C. W., minister at Hanóver, to the accomplished Miss Phoebe Camp, of New-Ark. W. Mch. 28, '92.

White, Ebenezer. In this town, Mr. E. W. to Miss Polly Barber [both of this town.] S. June 7, '94.

White, Hannah, m. Amesa Tyler.

White, Hannah, m. Ebenezer Richards.

White, Hannah, m. Dr. Redford Webster.

White, Jarathmael. At Dartmouth, Mr. J. W. of Westport, to Miss Alice Howland, of Dartmouth. S. Dec. 7, '93.

White, Leonard. At Newbury, Mr. L. W., of Haverhill, to Miss Polly Dalton, daughter to the Hon. Mr. Dalton. S. Sept. 6, '94.

White, Mrs. Lydia, m. Andrew Cotton.

White, Mary, m. Moses Brown.

White, Polly, m. Hugh Maglone.

White, Russell. At Danbury (Conn.), Mr. R. W., to Miss Susannah Burr. W. Apr. 18, '92.

White, Sally, m. Andrew Blackman.

White, Sally, m. William Clouston.

Whithead, Deborah, m. Thomas Davenport.

Whitemore, Joseph. Last evening, by the Rev. Dr. Stillman, Mr. J. W. to Miss Elizabeth Cooper. W. June 27, '92.

Whitfield, Miss, m. Mr. Collins.

Whiting, Abraham K. At Great Barrington, Mr. A. K. W. to Miss Wheeler. S. Nov. 23, '93.

Whiting, Charlotte, m. William Leverett.

Whiting, Samuel. Last Thursday evening, Mr. S. W., to Miss Hannah Hill. S. Feb. 6, '90.

Whiting, Sukey, m. Bathuel Boyd.

Whitman, Susanna, m. Oliver Allen.

Whitman, Thomas. Mr. T. W., to Mrs. Jenny Norcross, both of this town. W. Oct. 6, '90.

Whitney, Aron. At Shurburn, Mr. A. W., to Miss Ede Fisk, both of that town. S. May 17, '94.

Whitney, Ezra. Mr. E. W., to Miss Betsy Marshall [of this town]. S. May 31, '88.

Whitney, John. On Thursday evening last, J. W., Esq., merchant of the State of Georgia, to the amiable Mrs. Bridget Seymore, of Wesport. S. June 2, '92.

Whitney, Mrs. Mary, m. Col. Benjamin Hoppin.

Whitney, Silas. In this town, Mr. S. W. to Miss Polly McClury. W. Feb. 12, '94.

Whitemore, Sarah, m. William Borroughs.

Whitterfield, Miss, m. Mr. Smith.

Wickham, Eliza, m. Dr. Walter C. Gardiner.

Wicks, Sally, m. Capt. Benjamin North.

Widererfield, Betsy, m. Benjamin Spear.

Wieder, Christopher. At Green Castle, Mr. C. W., to Mrs. Margaret Hawson; their ages added together made one hundred and thirty-two years. W. Feb. 22, '92.

Wiggen, Capt. Simon, at Exeter, Capt. S. W. to Miss Joanna Thurston. S. July 28, '92.

Wigglesworth, Peggy, m. Rev. John Andrews.

Wigglesworth, Sally, m. Francis B. Belquet.

Wight, Rev. Ebenezer. The Rev. E. W. of this town, to Miss Katy Fuller of Dedham. S. Dec. 24, '85.

Wild, David. In this town, by the Rev. Mr. Eckley, on Thursday evening, Mr. D. W., merchant, to Mrs. Bryant. S. Jan. 7, '92.

Wild, Jonathan. In this town, Mr. J. W. to Miss Mary Ridgway, daughter to Mr. Samuel Ridgway. W. Jan. 23, '93.

Wilde, Rebecca, m. Daniel Farrington.

Wilde, Samuel Sumner, at Taunton, Mr. S. S. W., to Miss Eunice Cobb, third daughter of the Hon. Gen. Cobb, of that place. W. June 13, '92.

Wilkinson, Betsy, m. Capt. Charles Porter.

Wilkinson, Mrs. Mary, m. William Wilson.

Willard, Catherine, m. John Amory, jun.

Willard, Eliza, m. Joseph Whales.

Willard, Ora, m. William Hollister.

Williams, Abigail, m. Dr. John Bartlett.

Williams, Major Abraham. At Sandwich, Major A. W., to Miss Nabby Freeman, eldest daughter of Nathaniel Freeman, Esq., of that place. W. Jan. 11, 1786.

Williams, Abraham. At Stockbridge, Mr. A. W. to Miss Sally Tolman. S. Nov. 30, '93.

Williams, Capt. Benjamin S. In this town, Capt. B. S. W., to Miss Lydia Coates. S. Aug. 21, '90.

Williams, Betsey, m. William Hyslop, jun.

Williams, Caroline, m. Josiah Dwight.

Williams, Charity, m. Robert Morse.

Williams, Hannah, m. Ebenezer Heath.

Williams, Hitty, m. Ephraim Wheeler.

Williams, Jane, m. Cotton Brown Brooks.

Williams, Jeremiah. Mr. J. W., to the amiable Miss Matilda Davis, younger daughter of the Hon. Caleb Davis, Esq., of this town. W. Aug., 29, '87. She died June 11, 1793, aged 31. Notice W. June 12.

Williams, Jerusha, m. Ithamar Fairbanks.

Williams, John. At Gloucester, by Rev. Mr. Murray, Mr. J. W., of Boston, to Miss Sally Pearce, of that place. W. July 15, '89.

Williams, John. At Watertown, Mr. J. W. to Miss Rhoda Willington. W. Nov. 19, '94.

Williams, Mary, m. William Pratt.

Williams, Nancy, m. Rev. Mr. Smith.

Williams, Patty, m. Capt. Lemuel Toby.

Williams, Prudence, m. Rev. Bezaleel Howard.

Williams, Rachel, m. James Holt Leathesby.

Williams, Robert. At Cape Ann, Mr. R. W., of this town, merchant, to Miss Bethiah Pearce. W. May 30, '87.

Williams, Sally, m. William Deblois.

Williams, Thomas. Mr. T. W., to Miss Susanna Atwood. S. May 8, '90.

Williams, Timothy. At Roxbury, T. W. Esq., Attorney at Law, to Miss Elizabeth M'Carthy, daughter to the late Capt. D. M'Carthy. W. Oct. 26, '91.

Williams, William. In this town, Mr. W. W., hatter, to Miss Betsey Blake. S. Aug. 8, '89.

Williamson, Hon. Hugh. At New York, the Hon. H. W., Esq., Delegate in Congress from North Carolina, to Miss Apthrop, daughter of Charles Ward Apthorp, Esq. W. Jan. 14, '89.

Willington, Rhoda, m. John Williams.

Willis, Nathaniel. In Virginia, Mr. N. W., Printer, to Miss Mary Cartmill, daughter of Mr. Nathaniel Cartmill, of Frederick county—an agreeable young lady. W. Mch. 11, '89.

Willson, Hon. James. By the Rev. Dr. Thacher, the Hon. J. W., Esq., one of the Judges of the Supreme Court of the United States, to the amiable Miss Hannah Gray, of this town. S. Sept. 21, '93.

Wilmer, Simon. At Worton (Maryland), S. W., Esq., to Mrs. Sarah Crocket. S. Oct. 27, '92.

Wilson, Dolly, m. John Thorndike.

Wilson, Mrs. Sukey, m. Ebenezer Lealand.

Wilson, Susanna, m. Lot Wheelwright.

Wilson, William. At New York, Mr. W. W., Merchant, to Miss Agnes Kerr, both of that city. S. July 1, '86.

Wilson, Capt. William. At New London, Capt. W. W. to Miss Polly Clay. S. Feb. 9, 93.

Wilson, William. At Woodhouse, (Eng.) Mr. W. W., aged 91, to Mrs. Mary Wilkinson, aged 75. W. Jan. 2, '93.

Winnek, John. At Menotomy, Mr. J. W., of this town, to Mrs. Betsey Hower, of that place. W. June 25, '88.

Winnet, Polly, m. Joseph Webber.

Winship, Abiel. At Dorchester, Mr. A. W., of this town, to Miss Allice Shepard, of Dorchester. W. Oct. 24, '92.

Winship, Thomas. At Lexington, Mr. T. W., to Miss Anna Harrington. W. Apr. 24, '93.

Winslow, Isaac, jun. On Sunday evening last, Mr. I. W. Jun., to Miss Mary Russell, only daughter of Mr. Joseph Russell, of this town. W. May 14, '88.

Winslow, Mary, m. Henry Warren.

Winslow, Ruth Stockbridge, m. Rev. Joseph Crocker Shaw.

Winslow, Sally, m. Samuel Coverly.

Winslow, Sally Tyng, m. Samuel Waldo.

Winthrop, Miss, m. David Sears.

Winthrop, Thomas Lindal. Last evening, at his excellency the Governour's, T. L. W., Esq., to Miss Temple, Daughter of the Hon. John Temple, Esq., his Britannick Majesty's Consul-General. W. July 26, '86.

Wise, Hannah, m. Edward Curtis.

Wiswal, Elijah. At Norton, Mr. E. W. to Miss Nancy Verry. S. May 26, '92.

Wiswal, Oliver. Mr. O. W., to Miss Ruthy Angier. S. Dec. 27, '88.

Witherspoon, Rev. President. At Philadelphia, Rev. President W. to Mrs. Dills. S. June 18, '91.

Withington, Enos, at Dorchester. On Sunday morning last, Mr. E. W., of Brooklyn, to Miss Patience Leeds, of Dorchester. W. Oct. 15, '94.

Withington, Polly, m. Capt. James Robinson.

Withington, Ruth, m. Dea. Jabez Sumner.

Withington, Samuel. At Dorchester, on Thursday evening, Mr. S. W., to the amiable Miss Lucy Tileston. S. Dec. 11, '90.

Wolf, Sabina, m. Hugh H. Brackenridge.

Wood, Abiel, jun., at Pownalborough, Mr. A. W. jun., mer., to Miss Hannah Hodge. S. Nov. 30, '93.
See entry for Dec. 4, 1793.

Wood, Abiel, jun., at Wiscasset, by the Rev. Mr. Bradford, Mr. A. W., jun., merchant, to Miss Hannah Hodge, daughter to Capt. Robert Hodge, late of Newcastle. W. Dec. 4, '93.

Wood, Ann, m. Dr. Benjamin Starr Hoyt.

Wood, Capt. Peleg, jun. At Newport, Capt. P. W., jun., to Miss Betsey Warner, eldest daughter of Capt. Oliver R. Warner, of that town. S. Nov. 15, '94.

Wood, Mrs. Ruth, m. Rev. Titus Theodore Barton.

Wood, Ruth, m. Nathaniel Gorham.

Wood, Mrs. Sarah, m. Deacon Thomas Thompson.

Wood, Sybel, m. Wesson Bedon.

Woodbridge, William. At Newport, (R. I.) Mr. W. W. of Medford, in this State, to Miss Nancy Channing, of Newport. S. Nov. 23, '93.

Woodburn, Nancy, m. Dr. Samuel Rice.

Woodman, Phineas. [In this town]. Mr. P. W. to Miss Susannah Robbins. S. Nov. 3, '92.

Woodruff, N. At Litchfield (C.), Mr. N. W., aged 65, to Mrs. Umberfield, aged 46. W. Feb. 29, '92.

Woodward, Nabby, m. Rev. Samuel Kendall.

Woodward, Obadiah. At Chesterfield (Vt.), Mr. O. C., of Halifax, to Miss Cloe Steaples, of the same place. W. Aug. 22, '92.

Woodward, Samuel. At Charlestown, last Wednesday evening, Mr. S. W., of Roxbury, to Miss Louisa Hooper, of that town. S. Feb. 25, '86.

Woolsey, Margery, m. Robert Giles.

Woolsey, William W. At Greenfield, Mr. W. W. W., of New York, to Miss Elizabeth Dwight, of Northampton, in this state. S. Apr. 21, '92.

Worcester, Leonard. At Hadley, Mr. L. W., printer, of Worcester, to Miss Betsey Hopkins, of Hadley, daughter to the Rev. Samuel Hopkins, of Hadley. S. Nov. 16, '93.

Worthington, Frances, m. Hon. Fisher Ames.

Worthington, Mary, m. Hon. Jonathan Bliss.

Wright, Aaron, jun. At West Springfield, Mr. A. W., jun., to Miss Helena Door Breck. W. Oct. 29, '94.

Wright, Nancy, m. George Kirk.

Wyer, Mrs. Alice, m. Thomas Bartlett.

Wyer, Eunice, m. Joshua Swain.

Wyer, Robert, jun. Mr. R. W., jun., to Miss Lucretia Tuckerman [both of this town.] S. Oct. 23, '90.

Wyeth, John. At Harrisburg (Pen.), Mr. J. W., printer, to Miss Lucy Weiss, daughter of Lewis Weiss, Esq., of Philadelphia. S. June 15, '93.

Wyman, Simeon. [In this town] Mr. S. W. to Miss Susannah Edwards. W. Oct. 31, '92.

Wyman, William. Mr. W. W., to Miss Polly Wheeler. S. Aug. 14, '90.

Wyncoop, John. In Ulster county (N. Y.), Mr. J. W., to Miss Margaret Jansen, after a courtship of *forty-five* years. This *happy*, but not *hasty*, couple were between 60 and 70 years of age when united in the silken bands of Hymen. W. Jan. 25, '92.

Wynn, Peggy, m. William Rea.

Yates, Richard. At Coventry (England), Mr. R. Y., aged 88, to Miss Hannah Palmer, aged 69; infirmity and old age, was obliged to be conveyed in a carriage to the temple of Hymen. S. Nov. 10, '92.

Yorkison, Fanny, m. Ralph Patchan.

Young, Miss, m. Gershon Burr.

Young, Alexander. [In this town] Mr. A. Y., printer, to Miss Christiani Stutson. W. Jan. 9, '93.

Young, Polly, m. Francis Gray.